WHEN *words* HEAL

WHEN

words

HEAL

WRITING THROUGH CANCER

SHARON A. BRAY

Foreword by Martin L. Rossman, MD

Frog, Ltd.
Berkeley, California

For information contact
Frog, Ltd. c/o North Atlantic Books.

Published by Frog, Ltd.
Frog, Ltd. books are distributed by
North Atlantic Books
P.O. Box 12327
Berkeley, California 94712

Cover and book design by Gia Giasullo

Printed in the United States of America

North Atlantic Books' publications are available through most bookstores. For further information, call 800-337-2665 or visit our website at www.northatlanticbooks.com. Substantial discounts on bulk quantities are available to corporations, professional associations, and other organizations. For details and discount information, contact our special sales department.

Library of Congress Cataloging-in-Publication Data
Bray, Sharon, 1944–
   When words heal : writing through cancer / by Sharon Bray.
      p. cm.
Summary: "Based on her practice of leading writing groups for people with cancer, writer, teacher, and breast cancer survivor Sharon Bray provides a step-by-step guide for writing together—or alone—through cancer, from diagnosis through recovery, and defines a process for expressive and healing writing focused on an individual's experience"—Provided by publisher.
Includes bibliographical references.
   ISBN-13: 978-1-58394-158-4
   ISBN-10: 1-58394-158-4
   1. Creative writing—Therapeutic use. 2. Cancer—Psychological aspects.
I. Title.
   RC489.W75.B733 2006
   616.99'406515—dc22

                                             2006008407

1 2 3 4 5 6 7 8 9 UNITED 12 11 10 09 08 07 06

THIS BOOK IS DEDICATED

to all those

WHOSE LIVES HAVE BEEN TOUCHED

BY CANCER

CONTENTS

ACKNOWLEDGMENTS

This book would have not been possible without the contributions and support of a number of people. I wish to thank all the women whose voices can be heard between the lines and in the excerpted pieces illustrating the ideas and exercises in this book. They have kindly and enthusiastically agreed to be as much a part of this book as they have been a part of the writing groups I have led for men and women living with cancer. Thank you to: Rose Angel, Liane Aihara, Lillian Baer, Joan Banks, Peggy Bloom, Nancy Bowker, Susie Brain, Sally Jean Brudos, Paula Callahan, Carol-Lyn Conragan, Marcia Davis-Cannon, Barbara Dyszynski, Judy Finney, Julianne Fugloe, Carol Gaab, Ann Gang, Charlene Gibson, Ann Gifford, Helen Harris, Carol Hill, Shirley Holley, Judith Jacoby, Karen Jandorf, Nancy Jennings, Sheree Kirby, Laura Lenci, Penny Mann, Clarissa Magno Cua, Carol Martinez, Ceci Martinez, Pam Miracle, Genel Morgan, Laura Nugent, Irena Olender, Janice Peth, Margaret Prien, Janice Reynolds, Judy Russell, Candice Michel, Janice Schmitz, Debbie Snell, Carolyn Shuck, Neli Stascausky, Mary Jo Taylor, Kristen Thurston, Karen Usatine, Kathy Walters, and Hannah Walinska. Thanks also to those whose voices are still remembered but who are no longer alive: Jean Allington, Carol Braunshausen, Wendy Klee, Varda Nowack Goldstein, and Penny Warfield.

I also wish to thank the organizations that have generously supported my work and offered a home to the writing groups: the Community Breast Health Project in Palo Alto, where my first writing group began; the Bay Area Breast Cancer Network in San Jose; and the Stanford Cancer Center in Palo Alto. Thanks also go to Pat Schneider for her early mentoring of me; to James Pennebaker for his inspirational research and generosity; to poet Caryn Mirriam-Goldberg for her guidance as I explored more deeply the healing power of words; and to Ed Johnson, director of the Pacific School of Religion's summer session, for providing the opportunity to share and deepen my understanding of my work by teaching it to others.

My great appreciation goes also to Lindy Hough, publisher of North Atlantic Books/Frog, Ltd., for her enthusiasm for this book and for her wise and gentle counsel as it began to take shape.

And for the quiet yet constant support of my work, thank you to my husband, John Renner.

FOREWORD

The ability to tell and to listen to stories is one of the most significant differences between human beings and other life forms. Certainly other animals communicate to each other. Bees return to the hive and do a dance to tell their companions how far and in which direction to fly to get to the pollen-bearing flowers. Wolves nip, bark, howl, and growl to establish and maintain their relationships, and birds sing to attract mates and to mark territory. Whales sing to stay in touch with each other, and maybe to share feelings. But do whales tell each other tales? Do they interpret, analyze, or understand the feelings and thoughts that language can convey, and if they do, does it help them to understand themselves and their lives better? Do they use language in an attempt to feel whole?

Like other animals we use language to communicate information, but we use a particular form—the story or poem—to communicate and organize emotional information, and the ways in which we organize emotional information can make the difference between being stuck in grief and despair and finding hope and the potential for healing. *When Words Heal* will teach you a type of writing that is emotionally, psychologically, spiritually, and perhaps even physically healing. From Sharon Bray you will learn a healing method that has worked for many people facing serious illness, a technique that can evoke deep healing from within. It will teach you, in a gentle and structured way, to create a space in which you and others can write stories that convey the truth of your experience.

Writing in this way makes use of your powers of imagination and self-expression. Writing a story or poem of your own deepens your awareness of yourself as an individual. To tell a story you need to be able to remember the past, to imagine the future, and to connect them in a meaningful way.

This ability both to remember and learn from the past, and to envision possible futures, gives us great creative powers; it is the origin of everything that humankind has created. Our buildings, bridges, airplanes, cell phones, satellites, computers, poems, paintings, sculptures, contracts, medicines, and means of communications all began in someone's imagination. The human imagination has allowed us to survive and to thrive in an environment full of predators that can run, fly, swim, and fight much better than we can. It may even give us the power to directly stimulate the healing abilities built into all of us.

But we pay a price for this powerful faculty. Most of our worries, fears, and stress also stem from our imaginations. Looking back over our lives, and observing the lives of others, we become conscious of our mortality. Most of us keep our fear of death at bay for much of our lives, but when we are diagnosed with a life-threatening disease, suddenly that fear is front and center in our awareness.

A cancer diagnosis often precipitates an identity crisis. The shock and fear that may accompany the diagnosis can make us feel disoriented, afraid, and alone. It may make us want to understand, feel loved, feel connected, feel brave, and feel whole again. The act of writing down our story or writing a poem can help us reconnect with the feeling of being a feeling, thinking, and creative participant in our lives. When we weave together our stories and poems, we weave ourselves back together at the same time. The kind of reflective writing that this book teaches allows us to find—or as Viktor Frankl puts it, to *give*—meaning to our lives in the face of cancer's challenges.

Cancer is the bogeyman of our society, and even though most people (65 percent of those diagnosed) now survive invasive cancers, many people still believe that a cancer diagnoses is the same as a death sentence. Even when people feel optimistic about their prognosis, their treatments are often still difficult to tolerate, and patients are rarely left unaffected or unchanged. Writing, especially that which stems from the deeper self that emerges when we use imagery, can elegantly and powerfully express feelings, fears, hopes, and attitudes that help the writer find his or her bearings and inner strengths. This is precisely the kind of writing that you will learn about in this book.

Sharon Bray's method begins with a period of silence, reflection, and often the invitation to allow images, related to the topic of the writing session, to form. This technique facilitates writing from a deeper level because imagery, a type of thinking in sensory forms, is very closely related to our emotions.

Imagery often shows us how mind, body, and spirit are woven together. It is also a rapid way to get to deeper feelings and the thoughts that accompany them. Translating the multidimensional, emotional qualities of imagery into writing often greatly benefits the person attempting to cope with and make sense of the journey through cancer.

First, writing something down makes it real. You make concrete something that was intangible and invisible. When you write, you take something you are experiencing and make a mark of it in the physical world. As these experiences and feelings become more real, they also may become more manageable. You are given a chance to address whatever you most need to face.

The second advantage of writing your experience is that it makes it "reviewable." When you can review your journey over time, you start to see all the threads weaving your stories together, and as you revisit your experiences, you are often able to draw more from them. Writing forces us to translate the associational and emotional insights fueled by imagery and emotion into a more linear, sequential type of thinking, which creates meaningful story. Most of us feel better when we see our challenges as part of a larger story. A great deal of beauty and depth emerge from the stories that Sharon Bray teaches us to write. These stories will make you laugh, cry, grieve, hope, and appreciate the strength of the human spirit in the face of the frailty of the flesh. In the stories excerpted in this book, you will find courage, humor, grace, and persistence in the face of terror, grief, anger, pain, fatigue, and threatened loss.

Why would anyone want to encounter emotions of this magnitude? I remember years ago asking my colleague Rachel Remen, MD, how she could bear counseling so many cancer patients, listening to them talk about their pain and their fear, and she said, "Because it also brings out their strengths. It is such a privilege to experience and work with the strengths that these people have. It makes me appreciate humanity."

Having now worked with hundreds of people facing cancer, and having the privilege of working with them at the deep levels where imagery takes them, I now know what Rachel was talking about. *When Words Heal* will teach you how to gain access to this deep, soulful work we can all do when facing a crisis. It will teach you how to create a space in which your story and the stories of others can emerge. With careful instruction, Sharon Bray, a gifted teacher, empowers you to create a group setting where brief guided imagery experiences, or the reading of a poem or story, can serve as the seed that germinates in your imagination and then gives you a powerful way to express what you find there.

Exploring, wondering, stepping back, letting your thoughts and words flow—all these movements can help relieve the tension, the confusion, and the sense of disconnectedness that too often are a part of the cancer journey. Writing your stories, and listening to those of others, creates and strengthens your bonds to others in similar circumstances, to whatever you consider to be the spiritual element in your life, and most important, to your deeper self.

To me healing is about bringing all the different parts of you together in a way that sustains life and gives it meaning. Thanks to Sharon Bray, we now have another way to tap the wisdom we all have within, and to use it for healing ourselves and others.

MARTIN L. ROSSMAN, MD, author of *Fighting Cancer from Within;*
founder of The Healing Mind
www.thehealingmind.org

WRITING TOGETHER THROUGH CANCER

Stories are antibodies against illness and pain.

— ANATOLE BROYARD, *Intoxicated by My Illness*

In the decade since psychologist James W. Pennebaker first published *Opening Up: The Healing Power of Expressing Emotions,* expressive writing has taken its place among all the holistic, artistic, and spiritual approaches to emotional and physical healing. But the connection between writing and healing is hardly new: poets and novelists have used their writing to transform trauma and to heal themselves for many years. All writers, as Henry James said, start from "a port of grief." Writing, whether poetry or prose, allows us to say the unsayable, opening up our buried pain and emotions. Telling our stories unleashes our body's potential to heal. We begin to articulate the meaning of cancer in our lives.

Jean, who had been diagnosed with metastatic colorectal cancer when she joined my cancer writing group, talked said that her writing allowed her to explore her issues more deeply: "issues that exist because of cancer.... I am able to use the writing to stop my mind from fretting over the facts of cancer and treatment."

Writing helps us get through illnesses, trauma, or suffering, and even to get beyond them. Writing harnesses our imagination and liberates our creativity. Through it, we embark on a powerful and joyous journey of healing.

Writing about our deepest emotions and experiences can have extraordinary power and beauty. Writing alone or together helps us realize that, even in the midst of illness, our creativity and artistic self-expression cannot be quelled. "I now see," Louise DeSalvo wrote in her wonderful book *Writing as a Way of Healing,* "pain, loss and grief as the basis for virtually every act of cultural creation."

How to Use This Book

This book serves two purposes: to help you, if your life has been touched by cancer, to write through your experience of it and to give you, whether you are a cancer survivor, group leader, therapist, or healthcare professional, a process for convening and facilitating an expressive writing group for women with cancer. It is based on my experience of writing and of leading writing groups for cancer patients. It draws from and points to writing methods and resources available in workshops, bookstores, and libraries. I have organized this book around key themes and issues common to the cancer experience. Thus, throughout the book I address the reader either as a prospective group leader or as someone expressing her cancer experience through writing. Although oriented to women, men with cancer may also find many of the writing exercises useful in exploring their experience.

The ten chapters correspond to the length of a typical writing group series. Each chapter represents one session, with an overview of content, suggested exercises, and resources. I have chosen those I've found to be especially useful in helping individuals open up to their feelings and experiences of cancer. At the end of the book, you'll also find many helpful resources and references, whether you want to explore different topics in greater detail or to lead a cancer writing group.

While this book suggests a format for writing together, each chapter also provides inspiration to the individual writer. For expressive writing to be most healing, we need to get beyond our tendency simply to vent or to ruminate about a situation, instead constructing a coherent narrative—a story—out of our experience. By doing so, we can begin to make sense out of it and to gain a new perspective. The exercises in each chapter are designed to take you through the cancer journey, to encourage you to write narratives or poetry, and to help you reflect on the cancer experience—whether you are writing alone or as part of a group.

Writing Groups for Women with Cancer

Writing together through cancer is deeply joyful and life affirming. It binds us as a community of women with cancer and writers who express their artistry in words. When you write with others, the isolation you may feel when you are "branded" as a cancer patient diminishes. It becomes clear that you are not alone, that others share your feelings, and that what you feel is profoundly human. Knowing you're in this together gives you strength. There is solace in hearing others' stories about their journeys; the shared laughter and tears sooth our wounded spirits. Through writing, you begin to recover and exert some measure of control over your life, reclaiming your story and your voice. You bear witness to your own life and to each other's. As you share your stories and poems, you build a strong and cohesive community with others who are traveling the same road.

Only one requirement exists for participation in this kind of writing group: that you are a woman living with cancer. The motivations for attending a cancer writing workshop can be quite diverse. Some will simply be curious. Some, like Ann, may feel they have something vital to learn: "I wanted to use my breast cancer experience to learn more about myself," she said. Others, like Marcia, may love to write and be intent on using writing to explore their cancer: "I signed up immediately because I love to write, journaled through my cancer and my mom's. . . . I felt the need to write again." Some women may have tried writing alone, keeping a journal throughout their illness, but discovered that writing alone has not helped them feel better.

The journey from diagnosis to recovery or sometimes, sadly, to recurrence and death, is long and perilous. The women who come to a writing group will be facing the beginnings or aftermath of treatments—surgeries, radiation, or chemotherapy. It is a lonely and upsetting time. Some will have joined support groups. Each will be searching for a way to make sense of this significant life challenge.

Every woman will be at very different stages of the cancer journey. Some may be numb with shock from a recent diagnosis; others may be struggling with a confusing array of possible treatment options; some may be facing surgery or undergoing chemotherapy. Some women may be experiencing recurrence or a cancer that has metastasized. Others, who may now be cancer-free, may relish the time to understand what it has meant to their lives.

The decision to attend a writing group may be triggered by a friend's recommendation, by hearing of similar groups, or by seeing an advertisement from a sponsoring organization such as a church, hospital, or a cancer support agency. "I found a flyer at the radiology waiting room," Varda said at the first meeting of one of my early writing groups. "I like to write and felt this might be a positive way to deal with my cancer experience."

Whatever the nature of participants' specific illnesses or treatments, it is the cancer diagnosis that binds them. When I was first diagnosed with breast cancer a few years ago, another cancer survivor called to see how I was doing. As we ended our conversation, she told me, "You'll find you've joined a sorority you never knew existed." I discovered just how right she was.

Structuring a Writing Series

If you decide that you would like to design and lead a writing group for women (or men) living with cancer, first consider the importance of:

CREATING A TRUSTWORTHY ENVIRONMENT. The research conducted by James Pennebaker and his colleagues has shown us that certain basic conditions are needed for writing to be truly healing. These are fundamental to the way in which you structure and lead a cancer writing group. To encourage each other to write deeply and honestly about the experience of cancer, it's your job as leader to create a trustworthy environment, one that supports and honors the confidentiality of each person.

ENCOURAGING STORY. Research has also taught us that the greatest health benefits of writing are reaped when people write a "coherent" story—one that involves structure, causal explanation, repetition of themes, a balanced narrative, and awareness of a listener's perspective. For writing to be truly healing, it is critical for us to confront our anxieties and problems by creating a cohesive story to help us explain and understand our concerns. It doesn't matter what kind of story we create, whether it is autobiographical or a fictional narrative. The more detailed, organized, vivid, and lucid our writing is, the greater will be the benefits to our health. The exercises suggested for each session encourage this kind of writing. When we write together and read our work aloud, story creation—and the appreciation of listeners—is reinforced.

SETTING EIGHT TO TEN SESSIONS. I have found that structuring a cancer writing program around eight to ten sessions usually works best, depending on the sponsoring agency's calendar. Given the impact of diagnosis, treatment, and recovery, ten meetings give us time to work through the major themes that emerge during the cancer journey. The community of support that develops over the ten sessions is also an important part of the healing process.

CREATING TERM LIMITS. Can a group write together for longer than one eight-to-ten-session series? Yes, of course, but the length of the series will likely be dictated by two factors: the number of new cancer patients at each new series, and the health of the group members. For example, the cancer writing groups I lead are offered free to cancer patients or survivors from the sponsoring organization. As the programs developed, we needed to set term limits to make room for members newly diagnosed with cancer. Now a process of gradual transition from the writing groups is in place, so that there is always room for new members. If anyone suffers a recurrence, they are welcomed back into the group at any time.

Term limits serve another important purpose. A cancer writing group is not meant to reinforce a lifelong cancer identity. It exists to help its members express their experience of cancer and to facilitate reentry into a whole life.

MEETING WEEKLY OR BIWEEKLY. The writing group can meet weekly or on alternate weeks, running for about two hours. Radiation, chemotherapy, and recovery from surgery all take their toll on the body, so the women may have diminished energy. Two hours is a comfortable length for most and allows time for two writing exercises each session, followed by participants' reading and response. Ten to twelve participants are an optimal number. You may want to allow as many as fourteen or fifteen to attend the first meeting. Although treatment does take its toll, it's important to encourage participants to attend as regularly as they can. Typically, I've found that my groups average ten to twelve attendees each week.

FUNDING AND FEES. Every cancer writing group I lead at community or healthcare organizations is offered as a free service to clients or patients of the sponsoring agency. When I first began to lead writing groups for women with cancer, I offered the series pro bono to nonprofit organizations in order to develop the program and to demonstrate its value. After the first series, the writing program became a regular part of the agency's programs and services. Funding for the writing series has since been supported by grants and private donations obtained as part of the agency's fund-raising efforts. You may wish to charge a nominal fee to cover photocopying and other expenses. Asking for a small fee may also help to reinforce commitment to the writing series.

PREPARING FOR THE SESSION. Always arrive fifteen or twenty minutes ahead of your participants to set up. Arrange chairs in a circle or around a table. Distribute any handouts before the session, placing them on each person's chair. Make sure that name tags, pens, and extra paper are always available. Setting up gets easier as the weeks progress and you find your rhythm. Always allow yourself enough time to feel prepared and to greet your group members in a relaxed, calm manner.

The flyers I use to advertise my writing groups state that writing through cancer can be healing, but I am careful to clarify my terms. I also state that writing doesn't cure us of cancer, although some research suggests that it can have a positive impact on immune system functioning. Writing does help to heal our wounded spirits, however, and a positive attitude is key to healing the body. When our emotional outlook improves, so does our physical health.

Resources for Leading a Cancer Writing Group

Many resources and approaches are available for you to use in leading cancer writing groups. These include the research on expressive writing and healing; approaches to healing imagery and cancer support groups; and training in writing group methods such Amherst Writers & Artists, the National Association for Poetry Therapy, or guided journaling, among others. Goddard College offers a master's degree in Transformative Language Arts, which provides exposure to and exploration of the many approaches to healing through language arts. Additionally, the National Cancer Institute is a source of considerable information about all types of cancers, and its website has a section devoted to the most common cancers in women. Many resources are listed in the bibliography of this book, but they reflect only a portion of what is available.

Creating a Culture of Safety and Support

When you begin to write about the experience of cancer, all you may need to open up the emotional abyss of diagnosis, the agony of chemotherapy, or your grief over a lost breast, is a nudge from a word or an image. Acknowledging and translating our feelings into words is the first step toward healing. The second is to bring them into the open, to read our words aloud, and to be witnessed by others on the same journey. It is the job of the group leader to establish consistent group processes for creating and sustaining an atmosphere of safety and support.

The shared cancer experience defines a writing group in a unique way. Not only do participants come to write creatively, they also wish to use writing as of way to confront the reality of cancer and their feelings about it. It is a time of confusion, emotional upheaval, and vulnerability. During the first group meeting it is crucial to define the practices that will create safety for each person. Safety allows our creativity to flourish, but it also enables our writing to become truly healing.

Marcia, who has written in a breast cancer group, described the importance of establishing a safe environment, one that "really enables people to open up their deeper feelings. The affirmation and shared emotions build a swift intimacy that makes it acceptable to reveal anything."

How do you create the culture of safety in the writing group? A few basic practices are common to all healing writing methodologies. My own have been deeply influenced by the pioneering research of James Pennebaker and the well-articulated techniques of the Amherst Writers & Artists. Practitioners in the cancer community, among them David Spiegel (coauthor of *Group Therapy for Cancer Patients*), Martin Rossman (author of *Fighting Cancer from Within*), Lawrence LeShan (author of *Cancer as a Turning Point*), and Jean Shinoda Bolen (author of *Close to the Bone*) have also contributed to my understanding. The practices are simple and straightforward, but their consistent use ensures an environment where group members can open up and write from their deepest and most creative selves. The practices also help to keep the writing group functioning smoothly over time.

Basic Group Practices

THE WRITING GROUP IS FOCUSED ON THE EXPLORATION OF THE CANCER JOURNEY. The shared journey of cancer defines the writing group and is the reason for its existence. Group members have the opportunity to explore and confront their cancer experience through creative and expressive writing, even though the craft of writing is not emphasized. It is important to be clear about expectations at the beginning, including the fact that as each woman puts cancer behind her, she will transition out of the writing group.

EVERYTHING WRITTEN IS CONFIDENTIAL. Whatever is written and shared within the group is confidential; it stays in the group. Participants need the freedom to explore the full range of emotions that accompanies painful events such as cancer. As leader, you must maintain the safety for each person by protecting confidentiality and providing support.

EVERYONE'S CREATIVE EXPRESSION IS TO BE HONORED. A trustworthy setting also means that people can write honestly and deeply and know that their writing is taken seriously. Each person's experience and self-expression are unique. There is no right or wrong, no good or bad. Honor the beauty in everyone's words and stories.

A SPIRIT OF EQUALITY IS MAINTAINED WHEN MEMBERS WRITE WITH IMMEDIACY. Your group members will be writing together in the moment and then reading aloud what they have created during the session. Their writing outside the group is not shared aloud without the permission of the group, and never in the time reserved for writing together. As leader, you facilitate the session and write along with your group members, reading aloud at least once each evening. By doing this, you making yourself as open and vulnerable as everyone else.

THERE IS NO REQUIREMENT TO READ ALOUD. It takes courage to read aloud, and it is always up to each person whether she wants to share her writing with the group. Once you have written in response to an exercise, invite participants to read aloud, acknowledging that anyone can pass at any time. Sometimes an exercise you offer may be too difficult or uncomfortable for someone. Always give permission for members to write about whatever they wish. The most important thing is to encourage everyone to write.

MEMBERS ARE GIVEN SPECIFIC EXAMPLES OF THEIR WRITING'S STRENGTHS AND BEAUTY. The writing done in the group is new and spontaneous. Protect and nurture each person's creativity and self-expression. Encourage participants to listen nonjudgmentally and with deep acceptance, focusing responses on specific words, descriptions, or passages that they find strong or engaging. Creativity flourishes in an environment of safety and acceptance, as does our ability to write honestly. Never question the writing or offer critiques or suggestions. In this way the group supports each person's unique and full expression of her experience.

EVERYTHING WRITTEN IS CONSIDERED FICTION. This is a fundamental practice in the Amherst Writers & Artists' method, and it helps to ensure enough safety for members to write deeply and openly, as well as focusing on the uniqueness of each person's writing. Even if the writing appears to be autobiographical, treat it as fiction. Respond to the writer as the "the narrator," saying, for example, "I liked the passage where the narrator described. . . ." Don't allow for questions, interpretations, or comparisons to one's own experience. Even though there is tacit agreement that everyone is writing about their cancer journeys, treating the writing as fiction keeps the boundaries of safety and confidentiality intact. Participants can take risks and tell it like it is.

THE WRITING TIME TOGETHER IS HONORED WITH REVERENCE. Writing is a spiritual act. For writing to be truly transformative—for it to heal—you need to treat your time together as sacred time, honoring the need for quiet, concentration, and deep listening to one another and to one's inner voice. By respecting the act of writing, you create a sanctuary that allows participants to discover their own truths.

When Emotions Overtake You

Strong emotions may overtake you and the other group members when someone reads aloud. Expressing the strong emotions associated with cancer is an important passage in writing and in healing. Equally important is your ability, as leader, to help the group stay focused and to receive each person's writing and emotions as fragile gifts. Don't rush to intervene or comment, "Yes, I know just how you feel." In this way each writer will continue to feel safe.

I place two or three boxes of tissues around the room at each meeting of my groups. Participants can simply offer a box of tissues to a tearful reader and give her time to regain her composure. If someone is too emotional to continue reading, offer to have one of the other members read for her. Everyone begins to discover strength in themselves in these moments of emotion, shared experiences, and the affirmation and support of the group. Healing also occurs in reaching out, responding to the power and beauty in each person's writing, and discovering a shared journey. "I have been able to explore my feelings within the warm and welcoming embrace of those who are making the same passage," Judy said of her experience in a cancer writing group.

The African American poet Audre Lorde echoed Judy's words in her book *The Cancer Journals.* Lorde died after a fourteen-year struggle with cancer in 1992, but she provided powerful testimony to the importance of writing and a supportive community of women in helping her confront her illness: "My work kept me alive this past year [as did] the love of women. They are inseparable from each other. In the recognition of the existence of love lies the answer to despair."

The Comfort of Ritual

Routine and ritual also provide a sense of safety and security in the midst of a life turned upside down by cancer. As Jeanne Achtenberg and her colleagues state in *Rituals of Healing,* rituals help give significance to life's passages. They are outer expressions of interior experiences. Through community and shared rituals, we recognize the power of those invisible forces that heal and transform us. Rituals also make the writing time a sacred activity rather than a social get-together. When you lead a cancer writing group, including small rituals is a comforting way to invite everyone into community, quiet and ready to write. Here are a few helpful rituals you can include:

THE CALL TO WRITING: A buzz of greetings and conversation dominates the first few minutes of every session. To signal that it's time to write, light a candle in the center of the circle or ring a small chime, inviting everyone to take their places and to become quiet and ready to write.

GUIDED VISUALIZATION: Imagination is a powerful healing force. Begin each evening with a centering visualization, which will help relax and focus group members. A visualization can also be used to introduce a beginning writing exercise, one you may choose to read "around" the circle without comment. You can ring a small chime or Tibetan singing bowl to signal the end of the meditation. These small routines help establish the environment for writing and become an important part of each session.

BREAKING BREAD TOGETHER: If you have time, offer a short break midway through the session. In some of my groups, the members share the responsibility of bringing snacks. Breaking bread together encourages community and provides a chance for group members to offer support and encouragement to those who are facing new challenges, such as radiation or surgery.

A CLOSING CIRCLE: I like to close each session with a poem or short reading. An uplifting and inspirational piece works best. After the reading, join hands to form a circle. A closing circle provides you with an opportunity to express gratitude for the writing or to offer prayers or support for those facing treatments, surgeries, or tests. This act honors the women as a circle of friends traveling together. As the weeks progress, it becomes a sacred circle, acknowledging, as Julia Cameron wrote, that "art is an act of the soul." As you help each other find your creative voices, the group becomes a spiritual and supportive community, bound together in the shared experience of cancer. You begin the journey from woundedness into wholeness.

General Format for a Writing Group Meeting

A CALL TO WRITING *(lighting a candle, ringing a chime)*

A GUIDED VISUALIZATION AND SHORT FREE WRITE

FIRST EXERCISE *(usually lasting twenty minutes)*

A SHORT BREAK

SECOND EXERCISE *(usually lasting twenty minutes)*

A SELECTED POEM TO END THE MEETING

A CLOSING CIRCLE OF GRATITUDE

CHAPTER ONE

WRITING TOGETHER FOR THE FIRST TIME

*I am not sure where I read about the workshop, but it leapt off the page,
and I called immediately to enroll. I thought it sounded exactly right as
a therapy for working out the life-changing nature of my diagnosis.*

— JEAN, *cancer writing group member*

It's the first meeting of a new writing group for women living with cancer. There
are new faces, new experiences, and yet, the familiar: each woman who attends
is living with cancer. You share the journey, and yet each person is traveling a
unique road. No matter how many writing groups I lead, as I begin a new series,
I always wonder what the many weeks of writing together will bring.

As you begin the session, you may notice a mixture of curiosity and nervousness. Your own nerves might tighten a little; mine always do. Relax, take a
deep breath, and begin, welcoming everyone and introducing yourself as the
group leader, a guide in exploring cancer through writing.

Writing together will be a new experience for many women attending a
writing group for the first time. You'll want to establish a quiet, relaxed atmosphere for everyone right away and to create a sense of support and safety. I like
to begin my sessions with a guided meditation as a way to invite participants
into writing. Many resources and scripts for guided meditations can be found
in bookstores and libraries. As you feel more comfortable, you will want to
create your own. Below I offer a guided meditation to help everyone relax at
the introductory writing session.

Guided Visualization: Opening Up to Writing

Let's begin by getting comfortable in our chairs and, if you like, closing your eyes or soft-focusing on a spot in front of you. Allow yourself to take a few deep breaths, in and out, letting the length of your in-breath equal the length of the out-breath. Breathe slowly, deeply, feeling the gentle rhythm of your breath, feeling your lungs expanding to receive the oxygen you breathe in and contracting to release the old, used air. With the out-breath, let go of the tensions, worries, and stresses you've carried with you during the day. Feel yourself solid with the chair and floor, and notice how your body begins to relax. Begin with your feet, moving up your calves, your thighs, and your abdomen. Feel your spine strong against the back of the chair, and notice your shoulders—perhaps you need to stretch them, roll them a little. Feel them relax with the rest of your body. Move into your arms, traveling down to your hands and fingers. These are the fingers that will transport the memories and images residing deep within you and will bring them to life on paper. Let yourself feel gratitude for your fingers and for the rest of your body. And for a few moments, just let your body rest, relax, and open itself up to release the artist within you. When you are ready, begin to return from within your body to this room and the community of women who have come together to write and share their stories of cancer.

Getting Acquainted

Even if you are comfortable with writing as a means of self-expression, writing together in the context of cancer produces a little anxiety for everyone. Your goals for the first meeting are to put each person at ease, to acquaint group members with each other, and to introduce the writing process. Begin by presenting simple exercises that encourage everyone to write and to read aloud at least once during the meeting.

Start with a brief introductory exercise such as the one below, which I learned from Maxine Hong Kingston, author of *The Woman Warrior,* in one of her writing workshops. Not only does it help everyone get acquainted, it immediately engages them in telling a story about themselves to someone else and reduces any timidity about sharing one's stories aloud.

This exercise has three steps. First, divide the group into pairs. Give each person two minutes to tell her partner about herself: her name, the nature of her cancer, how long since she's been diagnosed, her occupation and interests, her hopes and expectations for the writing group, and anything else she might want to include. Instruct the partners to listen attentively without asking questions. At the end of two minutes, switch roles.

In the second step, instruct the pairs to repeat what they heard to each other in as much detail as possible, for example, "You told me that you are a mother of triplets," allowing one minute for each speaker.

In the final step, each person will introduce her partner to the group by telling what she has learned, saying for example, "She is the mother of seven-year-old triplets," until everyone has been introduced to the group.

This exercise serves several purposes. It introduces participants to one another. It demonstrates different points of view in telling a story: first, second, and third person. It requires active listening and paying attention to details—all-important in the act of writing—and responding to one another. It generates interaction, warmth, and laughter, helping everyone to relax. Now you can introduce the basic practices that will ensure a writing environment of safety and support.

Establishing Group Practices

The shared experience of cancer defines a writing group in a unique way. Not only are you exploring your creativity, but you are using writing as the vehicle for confronting the reality of cancer and your feelings about it. When you have cancer it is a time of confusion, emotional upheaval, and vulnerability. This first session is an important one, not only for becoming acquainted, but also for establishing the basic guidelines for how you will function as a writing group and create safety for each person.

Take time to carefully review the basic group practices together. I find it helpful to provide a short written handout that describes how the group will work, as well as the meeting dates and times. Revisit these guidelines briefly in the second and third sessions. Model responses to each person's writing so that group members can learn from them and practice their own.

Writing together and sharing your work aloud takes courage. Feeling truly safe takes up to two or three sessions for most new members. Timidity and apprehension are normal in the beginning, but nervousness quickly gives way to relief and excitement. "My heart is beating so loudly," a new member said at her first meeting, "that I *have* to read." As she began, her hands were shaking, but when she heard the affirmations from others, her face shone with delight.

Ann, a therapist and breast cancer survivor, thought of writing as "hard work." Fearful of not writing well, she came to the group determined to keep her writing to herself. Her resolve was short-lived. Ann began to feel more comfortable and finally read aloud. As she received the positive feedback from her colleagues, her reticence rapidly changed to unabashed gratitude.

Ceci shared Ann's apprehension but soon overcame it. "It was a bold decision on my part to allow myself to share my experiences with others," she said later. "It's very helpful to talk and write about our fears, hopes, and dreams, knowing that we aren't alone but are part of this universal experience."

While many may feel reluctant to read aloud at first, I find that by the third session, everyone will be fully engaged in writing *and* reading aloud, listening and responding to one another. Each has learned to trust the others and the writing process.

Now you're ready to write. Let's begin with an exercise that encourages everyone to explore her experience with cancer.

EXERCISE 1: TRAVELING THE ROAD OF CANCER

Living with cancer alters our lives forever. It forces us into uncharted territory. By writing, you have the opportunity to explore that territory and all it demands of you.

You'll need pictures of a variety of common road signs, easily obtainable on the Internet. These signs serve as visual metaphors for participants describing the journey through cancer. A metaphor is an implied comparison, one that calls up the language of our imagination and intuition. Metaphors are an effective and economical way for you to convey all that you feel about your experience.

Poetry is particularly rich with metaphor and provides wonderful introductions to many writing exercises I use in my cancer groups. For example, Nazim Hikmet's "This Journey" or Mary Oliver's "The Journey" are good poems to accompany this exercise. Hikmet describes a journey from a map that has been

drawn on ice.
But if I could
begin this journey all over again
I would.

If you use Oliver's poem in a group, ask a participant to read it aloud. Alternately, you can invite a group reading, with each member taking two or three lines as you move around the circle. Participants will nod their heads in understanding as they hear the lines:

and there was a new voice
which you slowly
recognized as your own,
that kept you company
as you strode deeper and deeper
into the world,
determined to do
the only thing you could do
determined to save
the only life you could save

Which lines in the poems do you like best? What images were most powerful or moving? Think about the images or metaphors you use to describe your own cancer journey. Call these out to one another, perhaps writing them down as you hear from others in the group. Now introduce the road signs one at a time. You have, for example, signs that read "dangerous curves ahead," "bridge out," "detour," "one way," or "bumpy road" for all to examine. It doesn't take much encouragement to invite everyone to choose one or more of the signs as a way to describe their experience. You can also use a metaphor of your own if you prefer. Write for fifteen minutes, then read aloud and respond. Remember that reading and responding take about twice as long as the writing exercise.

I've found that this exercise immediately engages everyone in describing their cancer experiences. One woman saw her journey as a one-way street, outside her control. Another described hers as a slight detour, a departure from the life she'd planned, while others complained of being on a trip they hadn't asked for, and only by sharing the road with others would they find their way home and to health.

Carolyn, who was recovering from breast cancer treatments, described her cancer journey: "[It is one] I did not plan to take, and which I have not finished, and perhaps never will finish. . . . It is a journey into that geography where reality gives vocal and disquieting evidence that you may not keep the promises you made to yourself when you were twenty. . . . It is a journey on a downward path that leads to the foot of one's one personal cross, the one you must take up an carry into your own heart of personal darkness."

EXERCISE 2: THE STUFF OF LIFE

No matter what prompt you offer, the fact of cancer is likely to make its way into everyone's writing. However, some participants may be less willing than others to begin writing about their disease. I like to follow the first exercise with a more general one, allowing group members to go in any direction they wish as they write. Old objects, used and discarded, always generate many stories and strong, vivid writing.

I still remember the first time I took a workshop from Pat Schneider, author of *Writing Alone and with Others* and founder of the Amherst Writers & Artists. She spread an array of old objects on the floor. Her comments were few; she simply asked us to find an object that captured our attention and write whatever it suggested to us. I picked up an old pack of Camel cigarettes and was instantly flooded with memories of my father, who died of lung cancer in 1992. I wrote nonstop until Pat signaled the end of the exercise.

When you feel a little tentative or stalled in your writing, using something you can see and touch often works best to engage your imagination and memories. Objects are powerful triggers for story. They stimulate our senses. They hold narrative and rich memories for even the most timid writer. Our castoffs—boxes of old buttons, an old doll, a wooden spoon, a man's shaving brush—serve as wonderful writing prompts. An old wooden spoon may remind us of our grandmother's kitchen or, as it did for one woman, the spanking her mother gave her when she disobeyed. An old rag doll may provoke the memory of a favorite childhood toy; a pack of cigarettes may bring back the familiar bulge in an uncle's shirt pocket. A golf ball may produce, as it did for Kristen, strong memories of her beloved father's own loss of his father: "Golf balls make me think of my father. Papa, we called him.... It was what he called his father. I never met my grandfather; he died when my father was eleven or twelve.... I picture him, blond and blue-eyed, in sturdy dungarees and scuffed brown shoes, alone, the only boy in his family, the youngest, running in the woods, avoiding the house, crying by himself, 'Papa's gone.'"

Paula picked up a set of jacks from among the displayed objects and wrote a remembrance of her mother, who had recently passed away: "My fondest memory is playing jacks with my mother.... She always had time for me. I knew she enjoyed our playing together. She'd show me all the little tricks."

As an alternate to objects, photographs are equally powerful as writing prompts. For years, I've collected black-and-white postcards from bookstores and card shops. Old photographic essays, such as *A Day in the Life of America,* found at used bookstores, are rich sources for exercises. Each image tells a story and inspires writing. For your second exercise, take fifteen to twenty minutes to write. If you're writing as a group, ask who would like to read aloud, and when they are done, encourage comments on the strength of the writing, modeling responses for the group.

Charlene was inspired by a picture of a Buddhist monk: "Your eyes search my soul and reflect yours. Falling into this space, my mind echoes back to you. What do you see in me? Why do I ask? Who are you I have chosen?... Quieting, I open myself to the shared space between us. You and I touch there, unique and alive, gazing into each other's eyes, reaching without hands, exchanging blessings for peace and happiness."

Pam looked at several photographs of women and began writing about her mother, remembering her before she was stricken with Alzheimer's. She addressed her writing to her mother, asking what she remembered: "Somewhere buried inside you is that beautiful woman in the apricot dress. Remember this? Remember how...? Remember when? Remember? Remember? Remember? But you don't. Like an old photo proof exposed to light, I watch as you slowly fade to black."

The Closing Circle: Love after Love

In this first meeting, you have introduced the key elements that will become a familiar and welcomed ritual for each meeting. To end the session, introduce the closing circle activity. Begin by reading a poem or a selected passage from a favorite author's work, one that is inspirational or offers a message.

For a first meeting, I often use one of two favorites to read aloud to the group. Both affirm the artist in each of us: "Purple" by Alexis Rotella or "Love after Love" by Derek Walcott. "Purple" reminds us that our creative spirits can be wounded all too easily:

In first grade Mrs. Lohr
said my purple teepee
wasn't realistic enough for a tent,
that purple was a color
for people who died,
that my drawing wasn't
good enough
to hang with the others.

In second grade, however, the poet discovers a loving environment in Mr. Barta's class. The poem reminds us that we can begin to heal our wounded artist with acceptance.

"Love after Love" is a gentle reminder to love our lives and ourselves:

You will love again the stranger who was your self.
Give wine. Give bread. Give back your heart
to itself, to the stranger who has loved you

all your life.

After the final reading, stand, join hands, and form a circle. You will no doubt see several smiling faces around the room. I always feel grateful for the gifts of story in those moments. I am reminded once again of the healing power of writing.

Suggested Format for Session One

Welcome and Guided Visualization

Introductions

Brief overview of the workshop format and basic practices

Exercise 1: Traveling the Road of Cancer

Write for fifteen minutes, followed by reading and response. You will want to reinforce the process of responding, for example, by referring to "the narrator," by listening for specifics, and so on.

Exercise 2: The Stuff of Life

Lay out objects on the table or floor. Give participants a few minutes to examine the objects, and then start timing. Write for fifteen minutes, followed by reading and response.

Closing Poem: "Love after Love" by Derek Walcott

Provide copies of this poem for everyone. Read it aloud, and then stand to form your closing circle and adjourn.

CHAPTER TWO

WHEN THE DOCTOR SAYS, "CANCER"

you have your own story
you know about the fear the tears
the scar of disbelief

> —LUCILLE CLIFTON, "1994," from *The Terrible Stories*

Guided Visualization: Diagnosis

Sit comfortably in your chair and, if you feel like it, close your eyes or soft-focus on a spot in front of you. Take a few deep breaths, in and out. Focus on making the length of the in-breath equal to the length of your out-breath. Let go of the day's distractions. Feel yourself begin to relax; feel the quiet surround you. Imagine yourself floating, hovering over the landscape of your memories. Gradually begin to settle into that place, that time, that day, when you first heard the words "you have cancer." Notice where you are—the room, the light, the colors of the walls. Are you sitting or standing? Who is speaking to you? Who else is in the room? What are you thinking as you hear the words? What are you feeling? Remember that day, feeling it again in your body. Stay with the image for a moment, exploring it completely. Now, slowly come back into the present, the room, and the company of other women. When you are ready, begin writing whatever you remember about that day. Just let your pen move across the page for five minutes. Let it guide you as you write.

Being Diagnosed with Cancer

None of us ever thinks that we will be diagnosed with cancer, yet we learn early in life to fear that very diagnosis. Once you are diagnosed, you are you are suddenly living in fear. Only by confronting it can you diminish its hold over you. In this second session, you move deeper into the experience of cancer, focusing on the initial diagnosis and the emotions that accompany it.

"Almost everyone responds to a cancer diagnosis with a period of shock, numbness or disbelief," Dr. Martin Rossman states in his book *Fighting Cancer from Within*. It's a lot like being shot by a sniper, according to Dr. David Spiegel, medical director of Integrative Medicine at Stanford School of Medicine. In *Group Therapy for Cancer Patients* he writes, "Cancer induces a special kind of fear," he says, "that of the body turning on itself, of normal cells becoming enemies and attacking others. It is a disease fraught with uncertainty and helplessness." Karen, a breast cancer survivor, agreed. "That I could have something growing inside me that could potentially kill me felt like the ultimate betrayal."

When you first hear the word *cancer*, it is a profound shock to the system. "It dislodges you," says Marc Ian Barasch, author of *The Healing Path: A Soul Approach to Illness*. "You look in the mirror, and one of the unfortunate ill stares back." You may be stunned and disbelieving, not even sure you've been struck by this disease. "Once the doctor said 'cancer,' I was unable to hear what she was saying after that," Paula said. "I was stupefied."

To others, you might even appear strong and composed. You sit across from the doctor, nodding your head obediently as if you understood. Yet, as you walk to the parking lot, you feel numb, your knees buckle, and the doctor's words jumble together in your head. Only later, as you hear the echo of the words *malignant* or *cancer*, do you begin to feel the heartache. Even during your best attempts to appear strong and positive for your family, other emotions creep in: fear, anxiety, sadness, anger, and loneliness. Suddenly your life is turned upside down. Your emotions swing wildly from one extreme to the other.

A cancer diagnosis is a significant and traumatic life event. Our emotions and accompanying questions about treatment are complex and, at times, intense. Along with the treatment that may be required, cancer can have a profound, and sometimes devastating, effect on self-image. You have become a "cancer patient" or "cancer survivor." This new identity is awkward and unwanted; you feel vulnerable as never before. "I was stunned," Barbara wrote, "still in my late forties and premenopausal with none of the risk factors.... I cried for days."

Living with cancer unites members of a writing group in shared understanding. You come face-to-face with your mortality and the knowledge that something alien and destructive is inhabiting your bodies. Curing it may mean fighting poison with poison, or even disfigurement: these are the horrifying challenges you face. Alice Hoffman, author of such novels as *The Ice Queen* and *Turtle Moon* and a breast cancer survivor, wrote of her illness in the *New York Times:* "Novelists know that some chapters inform all others. These are the chapters of your life that wallop you and teach you and bring you to tears, that invite you to step to the other side of the curtain, the one that divides those of us who must face our destiny sooner rather than later."

Karen Louise, a member of one of my groups, knew that the threat of breast cancer was lurking. Her sister had been diagnosed with it earlier; her family history indicated she was a high-risk candidate for the disease. Yet when she found a lump in her breast, she was unprepared. "The bottom fell out of my life," she wrote. "I was in shock and disbelief."

Ann, a therapist who had helped other women through difficult times, was disbelieving of her diagnosis. Her world turned upside down. "I lost a sense of control over my life," she said. In the poem "Breast Cancer in Paris," she remembers where she was when she first learned she had cancer. It eloquently reveals the terror brought on by her diagnosis:

All alone and scared
Wanting to whine
Be comforted
Held to someone's
Warm, copious
Bosom.

Will I die?
Out of control
Hopeless—nowhere
To hide from this terrible trap?
I can't cope with it.

"I felt I was falling into a deep, dark bottomless well," Janice said after being told she had cancer. "I had no way to stop—or even slow—my fall. I yearned for information, which I saw as the only way I could control the fall."

Early in your cancer journey, emotions run deep: bewilderment, disbelief, anger, and loss. "Why me?" is a common question. Kristen recalls hearing her doctor's words, "It's cancer," almost before she had shut the door on the way into his office. A mastectomy was likely. "What?" She exclaimed. "How can that be?" She awakened the next day, feeling it was a day just like any other before the realization hit: "I have cancer."

Having cancer feels like being betrayed by your body. It challenges your sense of self. Everything you take for granted is blown asunder. Shirley, who was diagnosed with lymphoma, remembers how, on the day after Christmas, she could hear tears in her physician's voice as she told her that "early results are consistent with...." Shirley's cancer was treatable, but not curable, and her choices for treatment involved risks. Later, as she described her ordeal, she wrote: "I do not like these choices! I do not want to be someone who must make this kind of decision. I do not recognize this life I am in. This is not the life that I know!"

A cancer diagnosis can feel totally overwhelming. Your world reels in confusion and uncertainty. "It was like a tornado," Pam wrote. "My life was being spun out of control with endless rounds of medical appointments and tests."

Hearing you have cancer can also feel like receiving a death sentence. It brings you to your knees and face-to-face with your mortality. Even in the midst of supportive family and friends, a diagnosis of cancer can be a lonely, terrifying experience. Candice wrote, "There is no lonelier feeling, nothing more isolating, than hearing that kind of diagnosis.... Even if the people who love you hold your hand, the pain and unpleasantness is all yours."

In the days after a diagnosis, you may awaken at night sick with fear. By the light of day, however, you try to be strong, try not to worry your partners, parents, or children. "I waited until after I had a needle biopsy and knew the extent of the surgery I would be having before telling them," Barbara wrote. "It was hard because I knew they were scared, and I did not want to burden them."

Writing about Diagnosis

How can you begin to express your feelings about of a cancer diagnosis in writing? A simple suggestion in a guided visualization like the one at the beginning of this chapter is often enough to open the floodgates. You might also find relief in just beginning to write about anything, letting your emotions find expression as they will. Often our feelings about our diagnoses are so close to the surface that the prompt is incidental. Cancer is not shy, and sooner or later, it will make its way into everyone's writing.

Begin with shorter exercises as you first begin your exploration of the cancer experience. Shorter writing exercises can be followed by longer ones, which invite fuller expression of your feelings and reactions about a diagnosis.

Writing from a Guided Visualization: Diagnosis

Try starting with the guided meditation that begins this chapter. As you conclude the meditation, write quickly, without lifting the pen from the page, for five minutes. Don't worry about spelling, making complete sentences, or punctuation. Just write without stopping. A very short piece written in response to a meditation will often be a passageway into a deeper and more powerful story or poem. After this "flow" writing, read without comments from the group.

EXERCISE 1: BRINGING FEAR INTO THE OPEN

Writing through the fears and shock of a cancer diagnosis can increase your ability to cope. Writing about having cancer helps you to externalize your fears and worries. Getting your feelings outside of you and onto paper allows them to be examined and heard. Your sense of being lost and overwhelmed diminishes. As you move into the darkness of cancer and express it, your writing intensifies, revealing your raw emotions.

For this exercise, use Raymond Carver's poem "Fear." The rhythmic repetition of the word *fear* in the poem stirs up the demons that accompany any life-threatening disease. Here is an excerpt. Try reading it aloud to yourself. Feel how the tension builds:

Fear of seeing a police car pull into the drive.
Fear of falling asleep at night.
Fear of not falling asleep.
Fear of the past rising up.
Fear of the present taking flight.
Fear of the telephone that rings in the dead of night

If you're writing in a group, Carver's poem is a good one for reading aloud together. Begin by saying that when we are diagnosed with cancer, one of the toughest emotions for everyone in the hours or days that follow is fear.

Have each woman read one line. Once you've read the poem together, read it again in its entirety. Which lines hold the most power for you? Write for fifteen minutes about your fears of cancer. You might try writing a list poem too.

Margaret wrote a list poem in response to Carver's. She created a vivid portrayal of her fears about her struggle with a very aggressive form of breast cancer. After she read it aloud, everyone sat in silence before responding. Margaret had expressed what many of them felt but had not yet been able to say. Here is an excerpt from her poem

Fear of recurrence
Fear of dying . . .

Fear of not finding a cure soon enough
Fear of missing the joy of living
Fear of pain
Fear of not seeing grandchildren . . .

Fear of never being the same person ...

Fear of not being brave at the end
Fear of missing life.
Fear of the nightmare never ending

Ceci wrote about her cancer experience in a short piece entitled "My Fear." Hers is a chilling description of an unwelcome guest:

You stealthily join me in my bed. You lay down beside me as I emerge from a deep, sound sleep. From the darkness and silence of the night, my heart is pounding as I hear myself silently scream, begging you to leave me alone. I wipe the warm sweat from my brow, but I feel a chill through my bones. You are the uninvited intruder into my life. You have raped me of my optimism and happiness. You are not welcome in my bed.

Expressing your fear and loneliness through writing diminishes their power. You begin to make sense of your disease and embark on the journey of healing.

EXERCISE 2: WHEN THE DOCTOR SAID, "CANCER"

"Poetry," John Fox wrote in his book *Poetic Medicine: The Healing Art of Poem-Making,* "is a natural medicine." Poetry can serve as a shortcut to emotion and a distillation of experience into the essentials. "Poems speak to us when nothing else will," he continued, helping us to "feel our lives rather than be numb." I like to make poetry a regular part of every writing session I lead. The beauty and power of the poetic images touch participants' hearts like nothing else. Poetry can give our own sorrow words, as Shakespeare said. Poems allow us to tell the truth and see our world in new ways.

Poems are wonderful prompts for addressing the fears and other emotions triggered by cancer. "Diagnosis" by Joan Halperin and "1994" by Lucille Clifton are excellent for stimulating expressive writing about your diagnosis.

In "Diagnosis," Halperin takes the reader into the doctor's office and the moment in the examination when she knows the news will not be good:

On the third of May
The blunt forefinger of a doctor
Pokes at a tumor
He says is in my breast.
His voice turns the new grass yellow.

Sucks in his bottom lip

Loads his camera with X-ray film

I can see dandelions from his window.

After you read the poem aloud, try to recall the day you received your diagnosis, whether in a doctor's office or over the telephone. Write for twenty minutes. You may want to begin with the words "when the doctor said . . ."

"1994" is one of several poems that Lucille Clifton included in her book *The Terrible Stories,* in which she describes her struggle with breast cancer:

I was leaving my fifty-eighth year
when a thumb of ice
stamped itself hard near my heart

you have your own story
you know about the fear the tears
the scar of disbelief

you know that the saddest lies
are the ones you tell ourselves
you know how dangerous it is
to be born with breasts.

If you're part of a group, read Clifton's poem aloud together, with each person taking a stanza. Read it again in its entirety. Take any of the lines you like in the poem and use them to begin writing. Allow twenty minutes.

Carol-Lyn was inspired to write "The Lymph Node Biopsy": "The hospital corridor is dimly lit as I am pushed on the gurney to the operating room.

I lay still in silent alarm. The panic deep inside me rising, but I cannot move. The burning of the medication hitting my veins is the last memory before awakening to the beeping of the monitors . . . I cannot escape the breast cancer diagnosis."

Closing with an Affirmation of Strength

I like to close each session with a poem that carries a message of hope or resiliency. When you explore the darkness and uncertainty of the cancer experience, it's important to remind yourself of the enormous human capacity for overcoming adversity.

"Survival Skills" by Kay Ryan is a great poem to read after writing about diagnosis. It conveys a certain toughness and strength, things we must find in ourselves during cancer and other hardships. Read the poem aloud as you end the session. You'll be reminded of your own will to live: "You know now, you were always a survivor." If you're writing as part of a group, then ask everyone to stand and join hands for the closing circle. Thank them for their courage and strength, for their gifts of words and story, and adjourn.

Suggested Format for Session Two

Guided Visualization: Diagnosis

The meditation is followed by ten minutes of writing.
Invite the circle to read aloud without response.

Exercise 1: Bringing Fear into the Open

Using Carver's poem, write for fifteen minutes, followed by
reading aloud with group responses. You may need to remind the group
how to respond to someone's work.

Short break *(ten minutes)*

Exercise 2: When the Doctor Said, "Cancer"

Using either Halperin's or Clifton's poem, write for twenty minutes,
and follow with reading aloud and responses.

Closing Poem: "Survival Skills" by Kay Ryan

Read the poem aloud, followed by the closing circle.

CHAPTER THREE

TELLING FAMILY AND FRIENDS

When you get diagnosed with cancer, every ghost and goblin of fear you have comes rushing through the rent that has been torn in the fabric of your self-identity.

—LAWRENCE LESHAN, *Cancer as a Turning Point*

Guided Visualization: A Conversation

Settle yourself comfortably into your seat and relax by taking a few deep breaths. Let your breathing gradually become deeper and fuller, noticing, as you inhale and exhale, how you bring in oxygen, fresh energy that fuels your body and clears your mind. As you exhale, let yourself feel the tensions you've carried all day begin to subside. Feel your body and mind begin to relax and your thoughts become freer. Let the images flow freely, feel the natural rhythm of your breathing, the gentle inhales and exhales taking you slowly into a deeper place within you—a place where you are safe and whole. Stay there for a while, exploring whatever presents itself to you. Now, imagine that off in the distance, you see a loved one, someone deeply important to you. You begin to walk toward one another. As you get closer, you can see the face of your loved one. He or she seems worried; perhaps this person is frowning, searching your face. You know you have something important to ask or to say. It may be a question that you have not been able to ask before now. As you sit down, take the hand of your loved one, noticing the details in the hand, the long fingers, the fine lines, as you hold it. Begin speaking, imagining that you are saying what you need to say.

Observe how you feel and how your loved one looks at you. Stay there with him or her a little while, noticing all you feel. Keep that image of the two of you, and carry it with you as you come back. When you are ready, make your way slowly into the room, into the space of safety. When you are ready, open your eyes and begin writing. Write for ten minutes. Keep your pen moving.

After Diagnosis, Then What?

After the shock of initial diagnosis, you confront an avalanche of information and confusing yet necessary choices about treatment options. Urgency is a common feeling. It adds to the vulnerability and stress you're already feeling. Even the information you seek can be overwhelming. The task of sifting through treatment options, dealing with contradictory medical opinions, and making the necessary choices can be as difficult to cope with as the actual diagnosis. How do you sort through it all? Where do you find the support you need to get through this virtual tornado of diagnosis, treatments, and decisions?

As a cancer patient, you are dealt a new set of social interactions, stresses, and demands that you've never before experienced. You face teams of medical specialists: radiologists, surgeons, oncologists, and technicians. Some may not have the skills to dispel your worries and fears. Others may contradict each other; still others gain your trust and confidence immediately. Along with your shock and fear, a confusing array of treatment options, and the dread that accompanies making treatment decisions, you may be consumed with worry about other people. What impact will your illness have on those you love, your family, friends, and colleagues?

The time that you must now spend in treatment—surgery, chemotherapy, radiation, and recovery—will change regular routines of social interaction. Your treatments take you away from work, school, and family events. This can be terribly lonely and isolating. Friends and family may feel awkward about your illness and not know what to say. It's hard to realize that their fears are not only for you but for themselves and their own potential losses. "No one wanted to believe it," Margaret said. "They kept saying, 'You'll be fine.'" "The word *cancer* makes people very uncomfortable," Kristen commented. "In fact, I think it is the thing people dread most."

Where do you find the space, quiet, and safety to express your feelings and fears? Writing together can help. In this session, the writing exercises will help you explore the feelings associated with some of the initial ramifications of cancer, especially those involving loved ones.

Writing the Guided Visualization: A Question for a Loved One

Telling your family and friends about your cancer diagnosis can be a significant source of worry and stress. "Telling my fifteen-year-old daughter that I probably had breast cancer was the hardest part of everything for me to do," Judy wrote. "I will never forget the look of fear on her face." Charlene acknowledged her difficulty in telling friends and family: "The last thing I wanted to think about in dealing with my own cancer was dealing with other people's fears. I told my closest family and friends only as I was able to face them.... I would spend significant time helping others adjust to my reminder of their own mortality."

Following a guided meditation like the one beginning this chapter is an effective way to address your concerns about how loved ones will deal your illness. After the meditation, write for ten minutes. Work on capturing the image you visualized. You may want to read aloud, but suspend comments for this exercise.

One former member of a writing group, diagnosed with metastasized cancer, knew she had only a few months to live. In response to the meditation, she described her teenage son's hands, bruised and bloodied from practicing on his bass. He was leaving that autumn for college, three thousand miles from home: "What I want to know is almost impossible to ask.... The question, Will you be all right when I'm gone? Are we making a huge mistake sending you three thousand miles away to college, when it's almost guaranteed I'll die just before you start or during your first semester? The answer? I don't know, can't know, until the time comes."

EXERCISE 1: AN UNSENT LETTER

Writing about your cancer experience is an opportunity to gain greater understanding and closeness with the people we care for most. Letters, sent or unsent, are a very natural way to communicate with the people we love. One of the greatest advantages of a letter is that we can write about our feelings without interruption from another.

How do you begin? Try writing a letter to someone you care for, someone with whom you want to share your feelings about your cancer experience. Imagine that person's face as you begin to write; you might even look at a photograph of him or her. You do not have to send this letter. Allow twenty minutes for writing, acknowledging that you may not finish in the time allotted. Continue writing if you wish, or stop at a point where you can continue the letter later.

Writing an unsent letters gives you the freedom to express all that you feel. Living with cancer may also bring back memories of other wounds that have not yet healed, and it may produce strong emotions. In an unsent letter, you can address someone directly, write from your heart, and express your truth. When you reread an unsent letter, you often discover new revelations and understandings.

Letters will produce writing that is intimate and moving. Strong emotions will likely surface. If you're in a group, give participants the opportunity to read aloud, but without comments from other group members.

In an unsent letter to my ailing mother that I wrote when I was first diagnosed with breast cancer, my feelings surfaced quite unexpectedly:

I have something to tell you, Mom, something to say. I don't want you to worry. I don't want you to be afraid. But Mom, I have cancer. Yeah, me: your big, tall, strong girl has cancer. Remember how you sat at my bedside all those years ago? Sat and tried to smile at me, tried to pretend you weren't worried? You told me that later, after it was all over, after I came home, that I nearly died then. But I didn't die, Mom and I'm not going to die now. I promise. It's just that the doctor told me I have cancer. And I'm having a hard time believing him.

As I read my letter aloud, I was surprised to hear my voice crack and feel tears running down my face—and yet, once I finished reading, I found the experience liberating.

Nancy wrote a touching letter to her triplets, beginning and ending with a reassurance: "You will be alright. . . . Even though I tell you I am not going to die soon, I don't really know that. No one but God really knows. . . . God was so good to give me three wonderful children. You will grow up to be joyful people. . . . My job as a parent is to teach you about God and about how to live. Once I have done that, my job is done. You'll miss me, but you don't need me. You will be alright."

EXERCISE 2: REMOVING THE MASK OF STRENGTH

We women are used to shouldering the burden of our family's fears and grief. We may try to appear strong and composed so that we can soften the impact of difficult events on our loved ones. The word *cancer,* when applied to us, sets intense feelings into motion. Those feelings can be frightening, not only to us, but to those close to us. One woman wrote about her cancer recurrence. When she read aloud, she tearfully described her husband's response as the oncologist told her that nearly all her lymph nodes were affected. "What does it mean?" he asked. The oncologist was silent. The husband turned to his wife and asked again, "What does it mean?" She turned to him and said quietly, "It means I may die."

Our partners, spouses, and family members may unintentionally communicate the wish that we be strong, because if we are, then it will help them deal with their feelings. This can add to our sense of isolation and become another source of pressure and stress.

Sometimes we may feel that if we control our emotions, if we act as normally as we can, not only will we spare our family the worry, but we might even control the progression of the disease. Dr. David Spiegel labels this mind-set the "prison of positive thinking." Yet that prison takes enormous energy to sustain, for when we awaken at night, the fears and worries we've subdued by day run wild. Beneath our controlled exteriors, our true feelings are begging for release.

In the first weeks after a diagnosis, family and friends may be overly solicitous. They may show their concerns through an outpouring of flowers, cards,

and visits. Yet when treatment continues, often for months, you might feel
that friends and family are less willing to hear about your illness. In turn, you
feel lonely and angry or then guilty that you feel that way. Where can you find
the safety and support to express all your feelings, no matter how conflicted
they might be? Writing together about them can help.

For this exercise, you'll need a supply of small Halloween face masks. This
exercise is a good way to combine writing with other forms of art. The entire
session can be focused on this one activity. In addition to writing, you'll want
to allow time for everyone to decorate a mask using colored pens, sequins,
pictures, small decorative objects, and words or phrases.

Everyone should have a mask. Think about how you put on different faces
for different tasks or for different people, especially if you are experiencing
cancer. Put on your mask and call out the different "face" each represents in
dealing with your family members and friends, for example, "brave soldier,"
"protector," "caretaker," "manager," "friend," or "organizer." Remove your
mask and write about the feelings behind all the masks you wear each day.
Write for twenty minutes.

Paula used a bright yellow mask decorated with tiny little black-and-yellow
striped honeybees. She told me later that she was completely surprised by the
content of her writing, something I often hear from my writing group members. Whatever direction it takes, invariably the writing reflects what they
most need to express.

"It was very strange because I intended to write about honey," Paula said,
"but as I began, I got angry and sad." She continued: "We have all felt pres-
sured to feel happy and for everything to be OK. Our families don't want to
think about it anymore—they want us to be happy and healthy. It is a great
burden to feel this."

Paula began with the lines:

Bees working furiously—hear the hum—making honey.
Fly little bee, flower to flower and back to the hive

By the third stanza, her tone shifted:

Bee good and don't make trouble . . .
Beehave—you must obey the ethic.
Put on your mask—mask of bee happy
                    —mask of team bee
           —mask of bee healthy

In the fifth stanza, she concludes with a revelation—and her honest feelings:

The mask helps the rest of the bees . . .
I cannot bee the cause of less honey in the hive.
They all need to feel safe and to know that my mask is on to stay.

ALTERNATE EXERCISE: ANOTHER POINT OF VIEW

Your fears about cancer are only part of the burden you carry. You also have to deal with the fear and concern you see in the eyes of your loved ones every day. It is hard, in those moments, to understand what they are feeling. In a poem that Joe Milosch wrote in one of John Fox's workshops and that was published in Fox's book *Poetic Medicine*, we are given a poignant glimpse of a husband's anguish and feelings of helplessness about his wife's cancer: Here is an excerpt:

when she's bald, lost the hair
from her eyebrows,
and lies with closed eyes,
with a skeletal look,
will you kiss her
and tell her
she's beautiful?

I don't know.

What do you do
in the bedroom,

when she is thinking
of death
and she cries?

I hold her hand, and I breathe.

Milosch's poem, when read aloud, also serves as a powerful prompt for writing. Not only does it deal with the agonies of treatment, but it also invites a different perspective of the cancer experience. Writing can be a powerful way to understand how someone else might be feeling about your illness.

One technique used in fiction writing is to explore the impact of the point of view on the story, writing from different characters' points of view. When we try to get inside someone else's head, it often helps us to understand how he or she might be feeling or thinking. Try using Milosch's poem to inspire you to write from the point of view of a loved one—a spouse, a child, a parent, or a friend. How might he be feeling? What would she say? You could even try writing dialogue between you and a loved one.

One woman, who wished to remain anonymous, wrote a description of an interchange between her husband and her, but she tried writing from her husband's viewpoint:

I found you sitting in your chair by the window today.

You had Susan Love's breast cancer book sitting on the floor. You looked out the window, your eyes red.

"Hi, Honey, what's the matter?" I asked you gently, not wanting to intrude. I was worried, but I couldn't let you see.

You smiled, that brave little smile that you wear all the time now. You said, "Nothing. Nothing's wrong. I'm just a little tired, that's all."

Then you got up and gave me a kiss on the cheek, avoiding my eyes. Walked away from me, that tight little smile frozen on your face. "Dinner's almost ready," you called from the kitchen. Then: "How was your day?" Just like nothing was going on. "How was your day?"

I wanted to scream. Really I did. I don't know how to reach you. I don't know what to do.

This exercise may be slightly more difficult than the others, but it can help to encourage understanding and perspective. If you use it, give yourself ample time to write, perhaps even as long as twenty-five to thirty minutes.

A Closing Poem: Injunction

Many extraordinary poems have been written for and by women living with cancer. The poem "Injunction" by Joan Halperin, published in a book of cancer poetry entitled *Her Soul Beneath the Bone,* captures a woman's experience of being told she has cancer and describes what she desires from her family. Here is an excerpt:

Inform the husband that I do not want my life measured
by time and obligation because I love.
Whisper to the children that I will hold them in my
naked arms
and spread my knees wide enough to crawl between.
Ask them to wrap their arms around my neck.
Sing me a song of such clarity I will know
that is only one of many Springs to come.

Read the poem aloud before forming the closing circle, ending the session on Halperin's note of hope.

Suggested Format for Session Three

GUIDED VISUALIZATION: A QUESTION

The meditation is followed by five minutes of "flow" writing.
Invite the circle to read aloud without response.

EXERCISE 1: UNSENT LETTER

Give the participants twenty minutes to write a letter to a loved one.
Give permission to those who are still writing at the end of the exercise to
continue writing or, if they prefer, to stop and complete their letters later.
You may want to invite reading, but suspend group comments
on the unsent letters.

SHORT BREAK *(ten minutes)*

EXERCISE 2: REMOVING THE MASK OF STRENGTH

You'll need a supply of Halloween face masks. Have everyone hold her mask
to her face and call out descriptions of the roles they have played or the
masks they have worn for family and friends during the cancer journey.
Remove the masks and, for twenty minutes, write about
the feelings behind them.

CLOSING POEM: "INJUNCTION" BY JOAN HALPERIN

Read the poem aloud or invite one of the group members to read
it aloud, and follow this with your closing circle.

CHAPTER FOUR

UNDERGOING TREATMENTS

There is a lot of waiting—waiting for the mammogram results, waiting for the biopsy results, waiting to talk to the surgeon and plastic surgeon, and then waiting for the surgery.

—JULIE CRANDALL, *Uplift*

Guided Visualization: A Healing Place

Sit comfortably in your seat, and relax by taking a few deep breaths. Let your breath become deeper and fuller, noticing, as you inhale and exhale, how you bring in oxygen, filling your lungs and blood vessels with fresh energy to fuel your body and mind. As you exhale, let the tensions you've carried all day begin to subside. Feel your body and mind begin to relax and your thoughts become freer. Let the images flow freely, feeling the natural rhythm of your breathing and the gentle inhales and exhales lulling you into a space of calm and quiet. As you become more relaxed, imagine yourself in a place where you feel a sense of peace: a place that is full of beauty, a place that is yours, private and secure. It is a place where you feel nurtured. It is a place of healing. Begin to fill in the details of this healing spot. Perhaps it is a beautiful garden, full of flowers; perhaps it is a mountain stream or a meadow. Whatever it is, hold onto the image of your healing place. See its colors, the quality of its light, and all that surrounds you. Reach out and feel all the textures of what you find. Listen to the sounds that soothe your spirit. Feel yourself relax into its peacefulness. Give yourself over to it; let it embrace you. As you hold that sense of calm, safety, and healing, bring it back with you as you return to this room and the circle of friends who share in your journey. Taking ten minutes to write, describe your healing place.

Can't Somebody Give Me the Right Answers?

Research everything about your disease. Ask questions.
The ultimate decisions are yours to make.
   —CHRISTINE WEBBER, *Uplift*

After diagnosis, it takes time to explore and discuss treatment options and to make the appropriate decisions. Yet decision making often comes with its own set of stresses. It may be several weeks before your actual treatment begins. It is a difficult and stressful time, and you may feel especially vulnerable. Each of us reacts in our own way. Dr. Martin Rossman, pioneer in using healing imagery with cancer patients, suggests that you gather your mental resources as quickly as possible to begin focusing on healing.

   Seeking information can also be overwhelming. It is a confusing task to sift through treatment options, deal with contradictory medical opinions, and make the right decisions. This time can be nearly as confusing and as difficult as the actual diagnosis was.

   Peggy was six months pregnant when she met with a genetic counselor and discovered she was at high risk for developing cancer, particularly breast cancer.

The genetic counselor and I calmly discussed the levels of increased risk I carried for developing various cancers—breast cancer being the primary cancer for which I was at risk.... Then we calmly discussed my options—to have my breasts closely monitored or to have a prophylactic double mastectomy. Then we watched my belly bulge and swell as the baby did a few somersaults, and then I cried for a while.

The fact is that I had already decided, before I went in to hear my test results that, if the results were positive, I would have a double mastectomy. But looking back, I feel as though that decision was made in a void. I had no idea about the ramifications of the decision.

Barbara agonized over whether or not to have chemotherapy and described her initial decision making as "tortuous.": "My oncologist said it was 'up to me' whether or not to take chemo.... My husband did not think I should do it, but everyone else I talked to encouraged me to. I scoured the Internet with the help of an old friend of who magically reappeared in my life shortly after my diagnosis. He helped me weigh the pros and cons and begged me to do everything in my power to help save my life."

Yet even when treatment options seem clear-cut, there are still many other long-term decisions to consider. Kristen, diagnosed with cancer at age thirty-nine, described her decision making:

My situation was not one with a lot of options, so my treatment was fairly clear. The decision would have been do it (surgery, chemo, maybe radiation) or don't do it—and not doing it was not an option I even considered.

I did have a few big decisions, though. The first one I faced was whether to have a single or double mastectomy....

The second one was fertility options. My oncologist wanted to do a lot of chemo—ten cycles total—and there was a very good chance I would not be able to have children after that.... And there was a definite warning against ever getting pregnant, due to the risk of recurrence. I wanted to know if there was anything I could do, any procedures, that would give me the option of having children in the future.... I saw two specialists, in addition ... to my regular team of doctors, and the end result was that there were no real options for me. I felt like I had done what I needed to do, as far as getting the information and learning what the options were.

Information gathering also helped Candice to regain a sense of control and to focus on making sound treatment decisions: "Once the initial shock had passed, and I was in the collecting-information mode, I found decisions very easy to make. My logical brain had kicked in, and it gave me the opportunity to be back in the driver's seat in my life, and not just a victim of circumstances."

OPENING EXERCISE:
DESCRIBING YOUR HEALING IMAGERY

Cancer, Rossman says, is like an athletic performance. The mental game, as top athletes know well, is just as important as the physical one. Guided imagery, which enlists the imagination in healing, is a powerful adjunct therapy for cancer patients. This technique helps the patient to relax, to reduce stress, and to relieve some of the debilitating effects of treatments. Using imagery can also lead you to vivid and descriptive writing about your cancer experience. "I had to see the disease as metaphor, interpret it, and act accordingly," Deena Metzger wrote about her cancer. "I used the imagination as a major tool for healing."

Carol, a member of one of my early writing workshops, suffered a recurrence of her cancer and faced additional surgeries and lengthy rounds of chemotherapy. She relied on visualization to get her through her ordeal. One evening, she suggested that everyone write down the healing imagery they used to combat their fears and anxieties during treatment. Here is an excerpt from a piece Carol wrote about the imagery she used during chemotherapy: "I am in the chair for chemotherapy. I see the clear plastic IV bag that holds the chemicals. My arm is outstretched, the needle in my elbow crease a straw ready to drink up the fluid.... The fluid is alive with floating bubbles of bright colors, small hearts, butterflies. These are the prayers, the good wishes, the love that my friends have sent to support and nourish me."

Jean, also struggling with metastatic cancer, imagined that as she breathed out, her cancer cells floated up into the skies:

Rising to join the Pleiades,
the birthplace of stars.
The Seven Sisters welcome these new beings
and become ten million strong.

Sending their bright blue light,
shining, illuminating my path
watching over me and blessing me,
the cells and I, each beginning a new life.

Penny, a dancer and a long-time participant of InterPlay, an improvisational group activity involving movement, stories, and song, visualized an InterPlay session: "It is the wounded season for my body right now. Even so, I know cell to cell, finger to finger, hand to hand, dancing bodies with dancing bodies.... Running, leaping, stretching past each other, holding still, but with that knowing ... we are still connected."

Use the meditation at the beginning of this chapter to describe your healing place. Alternatively, you can simply focus on the healing images that you incorporate in your visualizations during treatments. You can also be more specific and begin by imagining a healing garden. Describe, in as much detail as possible, your healing imagery. Without a doubt, beautiful and compelling images will emerge in your writing.

EXERCISE 1: IT'S LIKE READING A CHINESE MENU

How did you feel as you faced the decision-making process? What was it like to evaluate treatment options? Some of us take solace in gathering information. Although becoming informed about treatment options is often a good way to combat your anxieties and strengthen your resolve to heal, it is also all too often a very confusing time, as this next exercise illustrates.

Barbara Delinsky's book *Uplift*, which features hundreds of quotations from women on all aspects of the cancer experience, was the inspiration for this exercise. One woman likened her decision-making process to looking "at a Chinese menu." I found her comparison vivid, recalling my frustration at trying to understand the often incomprehensible cancer terminology and treatment options.

In this exercise, you'll use what poets know best, figurative language—comparisons or associations—to give yourself new and lively ways to describe your experience of making decisions about your treatment.

Begin with a copy of an actual Chinese menu. Imagine you're in a restaurant, and you can't read the menu. How do you make your dinner choices? Think about how you felt while you were making choices about cancer treatments. For just three minutes, write about how that process felt to you. If you're writing in a group, call out your descriptions to one another. Write down the descriptions that inspire you. Laura described the medical experts who gave their opinions as "prognosticators with broken crystal balls." Her colleague, also named Laura, described her experience as "swimming under water." Pam traveled "from one foreign country to another." Use one or more of the descriptions you've generated to begin writing about this process. Allow fifteen to twenty minutes for writing.

Jean, who endured a number of treatment cycles throughout her struggle with colon cancer, described her frustrations over treatment decisions as a "Face-off with a Pig":

My good friend Jim always said, "Never wrestle with a pig: the pig likes it, and you only get muddy."

I am facing off with a pig of a clinical trial, trying to make it a pet pig. I want to fatten it up, make it into a good eatin' porker, tasty and succulent, not too lean, nourishing. There is no time to waste. I am, after all, already sick.

In the ring is the medical establishment of rules, closed records, little lies, wasted waiting time, asking the wrong questions of the wrong people, people providing services as though they are dishing slop into a trough.

I am already sinking into the mud, having spent eleven hours last week and eight hours so far this week on the phone, talking, wheedling, cajoling for appointment times, reports to be sent, films to be read, and bills to be paid. . . . Information is doled out a piece at a time. . . . That doesn't count the twenty or so hours spent at doctors' appointments, taking tests, and having blood drawn. Then there is the time required for therapy and support groups to help me get through all this slop. Wrestling with a slick pig is a tiring experience—we're talking about a full-grown hog here—hard for this already tired body.

The Body under Siege

Treatments drive home the reality of our illness. For the two weeks after my two lumpectomies and before the beginning of radiation, I functioned in a dreamlike state of numbness. It wasn't until the technician began her precise measurements, creating the cast that would ensure my positioning, and tattooing four dark blue spots on my chest, that I realized I was not in a dream.

As I walked to the parking lot afterward, tears streamed down my face. It was the first time I had cried since my diagnosis.

For Pam, treatment was like the eye of the storm. "Once the treatments started," she said, "there was physical discomfort underlined by an amazingly calm acceptance of what was happening.... The external serenity masked my underlying fears, which came out at night in the form of deeply disturbing nightmares."

For others, like Paula, the horror of the treatment cycles lies close to the surface. She wrote: "What *can* you say about injecting toxins directly into your bloodstream?... What *can* you say about radioactive beams shooting through your body?... Are the technicians doing it exactly right each time...? Is 6,000 rads too much? You just hope, as you lie there, that the beam is doing its job of finishing off any maverick cells."

EXERCISE 2: IMAGES OF TREATMENT

You've decided on a course of treatment. Surgery, followed by weeks of radiation and chemotherapy, lie before you. Day by day, you make your way through rounds of treatment, fighting fear, pain, nausea, and changes in your body. What is it like to undergo and endure each prescribed treatment plan? What images come to mind?

Images haunt us, the poet Robert Hass said. They linger in our memory. They evoke vivid physical sensations and powerful responses in our writing. Images can even lead us to great insights. Jane Kenyon's poem "Credo" evokes a dark image of treatment:

Unholy ghost,
you are certain to come again.

Coarse, mean, you'll put your feet
on the coffee table, lean back,
and turn me into someone who can't
take the trouble to speak; someone
who can't sleep, or who does nothing

but sleep; can't read, or call
for an appointment for help.

Treatment is a very emotional experience as well as a physical one. Kenyon's poem is a good prompt for writing about it. Begin by reading the poem aloud or, if you're writing with others, encourage someone else to read it.

List or call out the metaphors and imagery that you use to think about your treatment. Use all five senses: smell, touch, taste, hearing, and sight. Read over the images you've written down. What do they tell you? Try using these images as the starting point for a poem or a longer piece of prose that describes your experience of treatment.

In the short poem below, Nancy lets us visualize and feel what it's like to lay stock-still during radiation:

I'm a snow angel, frozen
with a broken arm.
What are these
red, green, and white lights?
"We're ready." (Speak for yourselves.)
"Breathe normally." (I can't.)
"Don't move."
Okay, I can do that.
After all, I'm frozen.

Laura imagined a chain around her body, glued to her by fear and weighing her down. One evening, ghosts visit her. Here is an excerpt from her poem:

Link by link, they chiseled my chain.
In shadow they crept,
chipping more each night.
With each link fell something more.

A clump of brown hair
by ghost number one.
A lump of plump flesh
by ghost number two.
A layer of soft skin
by ghost number three.

ALTERNATE EXERCISE: CANCER IS A _____

Metaphors challenge us to see our worlds in new ways. Here is another exercise that always generates strong, vivid writing from participants. The process is simple. You'll make two columns of words for this exercise. In the first, use cancer-related words, such as *biopsy, diagnosis, radiation,* and *chemotherapy.* In the second, use ordinary nouns, for example, *sandwich, hammer, prison,* and *symphony.* Pair a word from the first column with one from the second, for example, "diagnosis is a hammer," and write for five minutes to elaborate on the metaphor. Write for twenty minutes total, and try to describe at least three new metaphors for the experience of cancer.

ALTERNATE EXERCISE: IMAGES OF TREATMENT 2

Some artists have created powerful visual images of cancer treatment. In his book *Illness and Healing: Images of Cancer,* Canadian artist Robert Pope, a victim of Hodgkin's disease, paints compelling and evocative portraits of people undergoing cancer treatment. The book is still available through used bookstores; if you can find a copy, you might find it useful to cut the book apart to lay out the paintings and sketches for everyone to examine. Little introduction is required. Study the images from Pope's book and select one or two that remind you most of your experience. Write for twenty minutes.

Charlene felt as if her body was being poisoned during chemotherapy. Her fear forced her to deal only with the present, and she visualized dancing with it during treatment. Charlene addressed her fear directly:

You grip my body when it happens. Wherever you came from, whatever the trigger, you claw at my heart and wrestle with my stomach. Suddenly in the dark place that goes on forever, you and I touch. We dance, you pulling me one way, and then that, me swooping around and under, pulling us both back upright. Balanced, your every move is counterweighted by my own. And then when I tire, my body slowing from jelly into stone, we sit frozen. You follow me into my mind and the dance renews there. My thoughts dart and twist, searching for safe haven.

Ironically, the treatments that bring your worst fears into the open and make you so sick can also save you. Kristen, who has endured multiple rounds of surgery and chemotherapy, described her experience: "One of the weird things about cancer is that you feel just fine . . . then you start with chemo . . . you feel off; your hair falls out; you can't eat; your skin feels weird; your body—it's all going wrong." But Kristen also spoke of the necessary determination to live: "You *can* get through it. . . . Chemo requires perseverance. You just have to keep going, one step at a time, one day at a time. . . . It's like an endurance test."

A Closing Poem: When I Inherit the Star

The deeper into the cancer experience you travel, the more your emotions will intensify as you write. (You may need to keep an extra box or two of tissues handy.) This is perfectly normal, and as you express your feelings, you will find strength and comfort. Close this fourth session on a note of strength and hope.

Lauren Alexanderson's poem "When I Inherit the Star," from the powerful collection of cancer patients' poems entitled *The Cancer Poetry Project*, speaks to the perseverance and new life that follow treatment. This poem can also work well as a group reading, with each woman taking a stanza as part of the closing ritual:

When I inherit the star,
I will pull the plug on these plastic lines
Binding me to a black-and-white hall.
I will paint my room

Until it smells of fresh lilacs,
And I will hang a eucalyptus right
Above your scalpel

At the end of the reading, stand, join hands, and form a closing circle. Thank each woman for her beautiful and courageous writing.

Suggested Format for Session Four

GUIDED VISUALIZATION: A HEALING PLACE

The meditation is followed by ten minutes of writing to describe your healing imagery. Invite reading aloud around the circle without response.

EXERCISE 1: IT'S LIKE READING A CHINESE MENU

Give each person a copy of a Chinese menu, briefly discussing metaphors and word comparisons. Before writing, describe aloud some examples of how it felt to make treatment decisions. Let them write for fifteen minutes, followed by reading and two or three responses per reader.

SHORT BREAK *(ten minutes)*

EXERCISE 2: IMAGES OF TREATMENT

Using Jane Kenyon's poem "Credo," discuss the power of imagery and metaphor and of using our senses in describing how treatment feels. Use, if available, pictures like those in Robert Pope's Illness and Healing: Images of Cancer. Have group members write for twenty minutes, followed by reading and response. You may want to limit responses to two or three minutes in the interest of time.

CLOSING POEM: "WHEN I INHERIT THE STAR"
BY LAURA ALEXANDERSON

Read the poem aloud, stanza by stanza, as a group, followed by your closing circle.

CHAPTER FIVE

WRITING THE BODY

I am still a woman
even if my heart hurts—
my whole chest aches
with emptiness, my soul sakes
because this body was cut,
one part off another
> —CARYN MIRRIAM-GOLDBERG, "Reading the Body,"
> from *Reading the Body*

Guided Visualization: Healing Our Wounded Bodies

Find a comfortable position. Close your eyes if you wish, and relax by taking a few deep breaths. Let your breathing slowly become deeper and fuller. Inhale to fill your lungs and bloodstream with energizing oxygen, and exhale the tensions of the day. Notice how your lungs expand and contract with each inhalation and exhalation. Feel their power, how with each breath they give you life, how they energize your body and mind. Sit quietly, and let your mind's eye travel over each part of your body. Begin with your feet. Feel how solidly they are connected to the earth. Gradually travel to each part of your body until you come to the part that has been wounded, the part of your body that cancer has assaulted, the part of your body that needs to heal. Imagine that you are a healer. You can dispense magical powers. Perhaps you bathe your wounded body in a warm bath of flowing water, soothe it with soft music, or surround it with a rainbow of healing colors or a gentle melody. Whatever your magical powers, use them now to heal your body. Feel how your body responds to your healing magic touch. Your wounded body begins to transform before your eyes, becoming whole. Stay with that image for a few moments. When you are ready, come back into the room, feeling the power within you to heal. Open your eyes and begin writing. Take five minutes to describe your healing powers.

Mirror, Mirror on the Wall

Dina Rabinovitch, writing in the February 2005 issue of *British Vogue*, summed up the dramatic change in self-image that cancer provokes in a woman: "Breast cancer has struck. And with it, the cure: chemotherapy that shears the hair from your head and razes your face of brows and lashes. And then the lasting one: the surgery that takes your breasts."

Cancer, no matter what kind, takes its toll on women's bodies and self-image. The side effects of treatment are emotional and physical: depression, anxiety diminished sexual interest, difficulties with bowels or bladder, swelling, or loss of hair or breasts. The body you once took for granted has disappeared forever, and with it, the image of you that you've held for so long.

Cancer treatments can drain you of energy and diminish your physical capabilities. Even though some of these changes may be temporary, you feel their impact on every part of your being. You've endured a variety of bodily changes. Your emotions are in tatters, a mixture of sorrow, anger, and disbelief. Before you may have felt control over your body and have taken pride in your physical capabilities. Now you look at the reflection in the mirror and see a stranger. "I had moments when I would catch a look at myself in the mirror and think, who is that?" Judy wrote. "It was very vivid and real—who are YOU? Who is THAT? . . . It was as if I was looking at someone else."

Your body has betrayed you. It seems alien and unfamiliar. You may doubt your femininity and attractiveness. With some cancers, the parts of the body we associate with being a woman are removed or reduced surgically. Not only do you feel angry when you see how dramatically your body has changed, you also feel great loss.

"My worst battle was adapting to the loss of strength in my left arm," Charlene, a massage therapist, wrote after her last surgery. "Instead of being my gladiator, leader, courage, and pride, my dominant arm was left handicapped and dependent, pleading support from my right arm rather than smugly domineering it.... I have grieved this loss more than all else," she said.

"Identifying and grieving for what has been irrevocably altered or lost," David Spiegel and Catherine Classen write in their book *Group Therapy for Cancer Patients,* "is a necessary part of coming to terms with the change wrought by cancer."

"I thought that I might adjust to not having a breast, but so far, I have not," Laura, a writing group member, said. "Living with one breast is, well, bizarre ... a constant reminder of having had breast cancer. I deal with this in the morning and the evening, when I put on and take off my bra.... I have not gone through a summer yet without my breast, but that raises a whole new level of issues around wearing swimsuits and T-shirts."

Karen described visiting a plastic surgeon after her double mastectomy. "Remember those cartoons of the scrawny guy on the beach who always lost the girl to Mr. Muscle?" she wrote after the experience. "Well, I felt exactly like that scrawny guy.... Talk about feeling like a pariah."

"The loss of my hair was worst when it was falling out," Kristen wrote. "Having it gone was less bothersome. I thought to myself, well, many people wonder what they will look like bald, and I am actually going to know." Kristen began engaging her imagination immediately to help her deal with the loss of her hair. "I imagined my hair falling out in big sections and making a tinkling noise.... That's what I imagined my hair falling out would be like and sound like. Tinkling bells."

Paula thought she was doing fine with the loss of her hair during her chemotherapy treatments. "Hair wasn't a problem. I usually wore my scarf or went 'topless' in the warm weather." Then she lost her eyebrows and eyelashes. "I felt faceless," she said. Paula's daughter came to her mother's rescue and took her to a makeup artist. As he filled in her missing eyebrows, Paula began to cry. "I never realized how important my eyebrows and eyelashes were to me," she said, "that they define my face.... Faceless—I've never felt that way."

When the Old Anger Strikes

Long after the experience of cancer is behind you, you may be reminded of it every time you look in the mirror and see the scars. "The scar from surgery is a daily reminder that I had cancer ... and the possibility of recurrence," Genel wrote. "Sometimes I look at it as a badge of honor ... most of the time I just don't want to see it." Genel is being honest. Those old feelings can sneak into our consciousness and catch us unawares as a momentary pang of regret, loss, or anger.

One afternoon as I led a weekly creative writing group, I read Marilyn Nelson's poem "Cover Photograph" to introduce an exercise to a group of writers. The poet describes how she wants to be remembered:

I want to be remembered
with breasts that never look empty
with a childbearing, generous waistline
and with generous, lovemaking hips.

In this group, we were not writing about cancer, but Karen, a cancer survivor, had suffered from a misdiagnosis and subsequent mastectomy two years earlier. She had begun writing, saying she wanted to be remembered as someone full of laughter. Suddenly, she put down her pen and notebook. As she reread the poem, the line "with breasts that never look empty" triggered a bitter remembrance. "I'm just too fucking angry to write about this anymore," she said as she put her pen aside.

When your body has been wounded, you may feel frustrated that you can't do everything you used to do. The old self, the familiar body, has vanished. The task before you seems nearly impossible: learning to accept the changes and love your body again. And yet you can. Charlene learned to accept her weakened arm as she reflected on her experience: "It will always tire faster than my right arm; its job has shifted to sentinel-for-stamina rather than gladiator-in-arms. It will always tell me when I'm getting tired, rather than carrying me when I need to be held."

The first step in learning to accept your body's changes is to acknowledge how you honestly feel about them. Writing can help you explore the ramifications of an altered self-image. Writing about your body and sharing your experiences can give you the opportunity to grieve, rage, and learn to live with the changes cancer treatments produce. Writing the body yields some of the most powerful feelings that you may have and inspires some of your most creative writing.

In this fifth session, you explore bodily self-image and reflect on the changes produced by cancer that you've experienced. This is an important step toward healing and embracing who you have become in cancer's aftermath.

Writing together about your altered bodies may take more than one session. Many exercises are available to help you explore your feelings about your body, whether through story, personal essay, or poetry. In this chapter, I offer several of my favorites so that you have multiple ways to write about an altered physical self.

EXERCISE 1: FINDING BEAUTY IN WOUNDEDNESS

I have always adhered to the philosophy that one should speak and show the truth, because knowledge leads to free will, to choice. If we keep quiet about what cancer does to women's bodies, if we refuse to accept women's bodies in whatever condition they are in, we are doing a disservice to womankind.

—SUPERMODEL MATUSCHKA, *writing after breast cancer surgery*

Images of cancer not only hold story, they also can convey a stark and unsettling beauty, as supermodel Matuschka's 1993 cover photograph in the *New York Times Magazine* and Deena Metzger's photograph in *Her Soul Beneath the Bone* illustrate. You've already experienced how images can elicit strong, moving prose. Actual photographs or paintings of cancer patients often convey what we are have found so difficult to say ourselves and encourage us to confront how we feel about our bodies after cancer.

Winged Victory, a beautiful photographic essay by physician and photographer Art Myers, portrays artistic nude photographs of thirteen different women, all of whom have lost both or one breast. Some of the photographs show women with spouses or significant others, but in each picture, the woman's beauty is revealed in her body and face with vulnerability, honesty, and even humor.

Myer's photographs visibly moved Karen, confronted with her own altered image after a double mastectomy. Here is her poem:

You offer yourself
Your nakedness, your beauty.

Yes, your beauty . . .
Your eyes meet mine.
You reflect a future for me . . .

Thank you for showing the way.

For this exercise, allow additional writing time. Lay the photographs out on a table so that each can be examined. Let each woman take a few minutes to study the photographs or paintings, and then allow twenty-five minutes for writing whatever the photographs have inspired.

ALTERNATE EXERCISE: PAYING HOMAGE TO OUR BODIES

By this time, you may find that tears are gradually giving way to laughter or even feistiness as you write and read together. The focus on cancer, while it never completely disappears, begins to diminish, and stories about other aspects of your life will emerge. For example, an exercise that uses scars or body parts as a writing prompt is just as likely to provoke memories of a childhood accident or your dissatisfaction with your hips, with the cellulite in your thighs, or even with the ears you've inherited from a parent.

The poet Lucille Clifton, also a survivor of breast cancer, has written wonderfully spunky poems about her body, including "poem to my uterus" and "to my last period." Her poems are especially rich as prompts to encourage

writing about bodies. As a pear-shaped woman, I love Clifton's playfulness in
the poem "homage to my hips":

these hips are big hips
they need space to
move around in
they don't fit into little
petty places. these hips
are free hips.
they don't like to be held back.
these hips have never been enslaved,
they go where they want to go
they do what they want to do.

Read "homage to my hips" or one of Clifton's other body poems aloud.
Have fun with it; her poem invites sassiness! Now write a homage to a body
part of your own. Write for twenty minutes. If you are writing and reading
aloud together, you will discover that at least as much laughter will be shared
as tears once were. This is a positive development; laughter, as Norman
Cousins demonstrated in his book *Anatomy of an Illness as Perceived by the
Patient,* is enormously healing. One woman's recollection of an unappreciat-
ed part of her body made us all smile:

*My father's ears were the objects of much family derision and humor. Whether they
were the result of aging or an unfortunate genetic endowment, we weren't certain,
because my mother took it upon herself to make my father's ears an example of what
we all feared. "You know," she'd tell us as we laughed about the protrusions at the side
of my father's head. "It's your ears that keep growing long after the rest of you stops."*

*We pooh-poohed her warnings, and it wasn't until I was an adult that I became
self-conscious about the physical inheritance from my father. While I was visiting
my brother and his family on a trip west from New York City, it took the honesty
of a child to make me aware of what my father had given me.*

I was sitting next to my ten-year-old nephew at the dinner table. "Aunt

Sharon," he said quietly, finally working up his courage to ask me a personal question. "Did you get Grandpa's ears?" I said nothing but with my free hand, brushed the hair away from my face to expose my ears. He stared hard, his eyes widening for a moment before he smiled shyly. "Yep," he said. I've never worn my hair away from my face since.

Cancer has begun to be a less dominant theme in your writing. Little by little, you are integrating it into your whole life story.

EXERCISE 2: THE STORY OF YOUR SCAR

Think about it. Every scar on your body tells a story. The scar on your leg takes you back to a summer camping trip and your fall over a protruding tent stake. The one on your forefinger reminds you of sneaking through a barbed-wire fence to pick blackberries from a neighbor's fields. When you see a scar on a parent or an old friend, like what Michael Ondaatje describes in his poem "The Time around Scars," perhaps you remember much more than a single incident:

A girl whom I've not spoken to
or shared coffee with for several years
writes of an old scar.
On her wrist it sleeps, smooth and white,
the size of a leech.
I gave it to her
brandishing a new Italian penknife.
Look, I said turning,
and blood spat onto her shirt.

Of course, there are the scars you suffer after cancer surgery, the ones that are constant reminders of how the disease has touched your life. In a poem entitled "scar," written after her breast cancer surgery, Lucille Clifton addresses her scar, asking:

and you,
what will you call me?

Her scar responds in a chilling reminder of its permanence:

woman I ride
who cannot throw me
and I will not fall off.

There are many poems about scars to choose from, and for this exercise, you might include Clifton's, along with Ondaatje's, allowing more range in remembrances and responses.

Think about the scars you carry on or inside your body. Remember that every scar has a story to tell. Choose a scar of your own and write about it for twenty minutes.

Laura was inspired by the imagery in Clifton's poem. She described the scar on her breast:

Ropey and red it climbs
out of the
dent in my breast.

It clings to my body
like a vine,
yet I can't peel it off . . .

It's the bad part of my body . . .
the part I want to
rip out and
start over.

Jean, who ultimately lost her life to metastatic cancer, wrote of the scars that everyone carries within:

None of us are unscarred.
There is childhood,
night fears.
Parents doing their scary but true best.
First love,
teenage angst.
Marriage, children, divorce,
separation, death.
Loss and scars,
scars and loss,
Life and lessons.

Carol, after she had recovered from cancer, wrote about her scar and how it serves as a constant reminder of what she fears:

The tips of my fingers
trace your raised surface,
sometimes probing,
searching for what was left behind . . .
Pain shoots through your center
unexpectedly; I catch my breath.

ALTERNATE EXERCISE:
I'M *NOT* A VICTORIA'S SECRET MODEL

I use this exercise to add some playfulness and fun to my group members' writing. Invariably, after they've responded and read aloud, we discover a true appreciation for our natural and imperfect bodies.

A Victoria's Secret catalog serves as the visual prompt. You'll find no shortage of photographs of scantily clad models with perfect breasts and bodies to present to a writing group. Without comment, lay the photographs on the table or floor for everyone to examine. Write for fifteen or twenty minutes.

ALTERNATE EXERCISE: I USED TO BE_____, BUT NOW ...

You may find that this last exercise is also a good one with which to end this session. It encourages you to look at your feelings about yourself before and after cancer. "We write," Patricia Hampl said in her book *I Could Tell You Stories*, "to find out what we know." How have your perceptions of yourself been transformed during the cancer experience?

Hold a small hand mirror up to your face. Look carefully at the person you see reflected back at you, the person who has struggled with all the ramifications of this disease. Think about who you were before cancer came into your life and who you are now, the person you have become. Write for twenty minutes. You might want to begin with the line, "I used to be _____, but now ..."

A Closing Poem: You Are Beautiful

Writing about the body will be an intense experience. You've delved into your feelings about all that cancer has wrought. Yet, you will also express a growing acceptance of who you are becoming and a sense of growing strength that reveals itself in the midst of the cancer journey.

For a closing poem, Caryn Mirriam-Goldberg's "I Want to Tell You How Beautiful You Are" is one I love to use with my own writing groups. It acknowledges that cancer irrevocably changes us but also endows us with greater courage, depth, and an unmistakable beauty. Caryn is not only the coordinator for the Transformative Language Arts program at Goddard College, she is also a Kansas poet and a breast cancer survivor. She leads poetry-writing groups for cancer survivors through the Lawrence Arts Center in Lawrence, Kansas. Here is an excerpt from her poem:

I want to tell you even this is beautiful,
and even the rounded flesh below, the silhouette
hollowed here, extended there, the shapes new
and sudden, the beauty you could never see
when they cut your body open to where
the breathing organs breathe, the beauty
you'll mourn from the other side of your life.

Read the poem aloud. It is enough to see women smiling and nodding their heads in quiet agreement to know that healing is taking place. You are learning you can discover beauty out of woundedness. Allow a few moments of silence, and then stand to join hands for a closing circle.

Suggested Format for Session Five

Guided Visualization: Healing Our Wounded Bodies

Follow the meditation with ten minutes of writing to describe your imagery. Invite the circle to read aloud without response.

Exercise 1: Finding Beauty in Woundedness

Let the group members take a few minutes to study the photographs from Art Myers's Winged Victory before writing for twenty-five minutes. You may want to limit responses to two or three per reader.

Short break *(ten minutes)*

Exercise 2: The Story of Your Scar

Use Clifton's and Ondaatje's poems. Write for twenty minutes, followed by reading and group response. Again, you may need to limit comments to two or three per reader, in the interest of time.

Closing Poem: "I Want to Tell You How Beautiful You Are" by Caryn Mirriam-Goldberg

Read this poem aloud to the group, followed by your closing circle.

CHAPTER SIX

FINDING SUPPORT

My support group has been invaluable in helping me face the challenges of breast cancer treatment.

—JANICE, writing group member

Guided Visualization: The Circle of Friends

Sit comfortably in your chair and close your eyes or, if you prefer, soft-focus on a spot in front of you. Concentrate, for a few moments, on your breathing. Let the in-breath become as even as the out-breath. Breathe in the calm and quiet of this space, the warmth and love within the community of women who are with you tonight. As you breathe out, let go of the day's tensions and distractions. Take a few moments to concentrate on the regular, steady rhythm of your breathing, gradually and gently falling into that deep well of memories, images, feelings, and sensations. As you linger there, picture a circle of people in the distance, all of whom you know. Move toward them, knowing that these are friends who care for you, who have helped you on this journey through cancer in some way. They are there to help support you, to hold your hand, and to guide you through treatment and into recovery. Come closer; see their faces. Study them: eyes, mouths, expressions— perhaps they are smiling. See how they open their arms to you. Move into the circle and feel the healing power of their love and support. Remain there for a few moments, taking note of each person and of how you feel in their presence. Let their love and compassion nourish you. Gradually say good-bye to this circle of friends, knowing that you can return to their presence at any time. Begin your journey back into this world, this room, and this community of women who are traveling the same path. When you are ready, open your eyes and write, describing your experience in the healing circle of friendship.

Finding Support on the Cancer Journey

"Serious medical illness," write David Spiegel and Catherine Classen in *Group Therapy for Cancer Patients,* "is a test of any support network." The journey through cancer lasts way beyond diagnosis. After the initial rush of sympathy and support, you may feel isolated, cut off from the rest of the "normal" world of people who do not have cancer. "There's an initial outpouring of attention and sympathy," Kristen said, "but then what? People don't know what to do after the first few months."

You feel different. You're now confronting an unknown and frightening future. Despite the support of family and friends, you may experience loneliness and fear. "I felt alone," a cancer patient told me, "even though my friends and family were wonderful." Friends and family may have their own anxieties and worries associated with your illness, and they may feel and act helpless. "My family was pretty useless," one woman wrote. "I did not know how I would get through this."

Charlene, on the other hand, found that the most difficult thing in dealing with her loved ones was her desire to remain independent. "Let friends and family help you," Nancy advised a group of cancer patients. "They feel helpless, and it lets them be involved."

Sometimes existing relationships change as your treatment continues. Some friends or acquaintances may distance themselves; others may come closer. Many people tell me they discovered their real friendships during the cancer experience. Your opportunities for social interaction decrease as you confront the demands of treatment. Even the people closest to you can become stressed during your illness. You may wonder if you've become a burden or if your fears and needs are too worrisome to loved ones. "I saw my mother . . . on my good days," Genel wrote. "I know she suffered silently as I went through everything."

Whether or not you feel well supported in your cancer journey, being part of a group of people living with cancer can diminish your fears and provide a source of comfort. You learn that what you are feeling and experiencing is not unusual. You may find that other cancer patients who are traveling the same path understand your experience better than anyone else.

After one woman spent an evening in her cancer writing group, her husband asked, "Aren't you done with that yet?" As she told the story to her fellow writers the following week, she said. "He just doesn't understand that part." Among those who share in the experience of cancer, it may be easier to express what we are truly feeling, because we don't need to protect anyone. This process can be liberating, even healing.

During the cancer journey, social support becomes even more critical in helping you navigate the stresses associated with your illness. Different stages of the disease may require several different kinds of support. Regardless of what form they take, social support groups can improve your quality of life. Whether formal or informal groups, they offer you a number of benefits: information, emotional support, and an opportunity to share experiences and to diminish the fear and loneliness that you feel during diagnosis and treatment.

When Candice was diagnosed, she went to a local breast cancer services nonprofit and "found a wonderful support network ... of women who were willing to share their own experiences of cancer." Paula wasn't going to join a support group, but when a friend convinced her that it would be beneficial, she decided to try one at a nearby hospital. "Our group had such positive dynamics," she said. "We have kept in touch ... meeting once a month for a potluck dinner. The support of the group has made a tremendous difference to each and every one of us."

There are many different types of support groups available through hospitals, community organizations, and national cancer organizations. Some organizations are listed in the resource section of this book, but most are easily found on the Internet or through your doctor or hospital. It's up to you to decide what's best for you, but cancer organizations offer a wealth of valuable services, including medical information, online support groups, telephone counseling, and even "buddy systems," in which a cancer patient is helped by a cancer survivor.

Writing Together as Social Support

Another powerful kind of social support comes from writing together in a community of people who share the experience of cancer. While a writing group does not substitute for a therapeutic support group, it does offer the experience of shared community and the opportunity for self-expression. Joining a cancer writing group is something personal that you can do as part of your self-care. As you write and tell stories with others who have embarked on the same journey, you can feel understood in a way that you might not elsewhere. "I feel I can be seen," Karen said of her group.

"I feel less alone," Judy agreed. "When we are in chemotherapy," she said, "we feel so very different from others. Here we can identify with each other. Everyone shares the same experience."

OPENING EXERCISE: THE CIRCLE OF FRIENDS

The visualization at the beginning of this chapter invites you to reflect on the importance of others' kindness to you throughout the cancer experience. Once you have completed the guided visualization, write for five minutes, describing what you feel or would like to remember about your healing circle of friends. If you are writing in a group, invite the members to read aloud without comment, holding each person's words in silent appreciation.

The experience of writing with other women living with cancer was an important aspect of Kathy's cancer journey. She began by asking the question, "Starting now, what do I want to remember?" Here is an excerpt from her poem:

A gathering of women
Discovering themselves
Sharing those discoveries
Delighting in each other's stories
Caring for one another.

Neli explained that writing together allows the exterior world to disappear and provides the safety to reach deep inside: "We manifest ourselves in wonderful voices: an outpouring of vibrant, multicolored art comes out. Sadness and happiness, darkness and light, pain and relief, warmth and cold ... laughter and tears. And at the end of each evening we part ... to glide: happy, fearless, ethereal and eternal? Perhaps ... "

EXERCISE 1: HELPING HANDS

When you have the time to be still and to reflect, as the act of writing demands, you can observe and remember the unexpected acts of kindness and compassion that you sometimes experience. Writing makes us pay close attention, move outside ourselves, and notice things that we might otherwise have missed in the frantic pace of our lives. You may discover that support has come from many places and people: a card in the mail from a relative, a telephone call from a friend, a child's handmade get well card, being added to a prayer list, a casserole delivered by a neighbor, a lift to a chemotherapy appointment, even the soft nuzzle of a pet, attentive to our every mood. Laura wrote to her cat, which, ironically, was also diagnosed with cancer:

Waiting for the pathology report.
I look around the apartment we've shared for the past twelve years ...
You sit now, curled up next to me, your eyes narrowing as you start to doze,
Unaware of what we're waiting for.

Finding companionship and support, often in unexpected places, helps you to feel less alone.

For this exercise, use a photograph of hands, preferably ones grasped in friendship or offering something. I've used a beautiful postcard of Tibetan women's hands for this exercise, but you can find good resources in magazines and in photographic art books. As you study the photograph, recall those times, perhaps unexpected, when someone helped you. Take just two or three minutes to list a few of those experiences, and, in your group, read one or two examples aloud. For fifteen minutes, describe one or more of those experiences of kindness, support, or friendship. If you want to explore another perspective in this exercise, try writing about a time you found a way to help someone in need and how it made you feel.

In a piece titled "Warm Hands," Karen wrote about discovering the gift of others' support during cancer:

Maybe this early training . . .
taught me to accept the hands that reached out.
Maybe the net these hands wove beneath my fragile psyche
was enough to hold me.
Maybe.

Maybe as these warm hands held me
I learned to trust just a little bit more.
Maybe they will be there if I need them again.

Debbie, recovering from a mastectomy, wrote about an unexpected gift of help from a group of fellow church members. When they first telephoned, she was reluctant to have visitors. She didn't want to have to entertain anyone.

"We'd like to visit you," she said.
"How nice," I lied.
"Would 11:00 on Wednesday be OK?"
"That's fine," I lied again."

Her initial reluctance to receive her guests vanished as the women arrived with flowers, homemade bread, and soup for her family's dinner. They talked and laughed, sharing their lives. One woman talked about her own mastectomy experience and showed them all the results of her breast reconstruction. Later, as they sat sharing stories over lunch, Debbie discovered one of her visitors out in the backyard with a shovel, cleaning up after her dog! "I was so wrong. These were not church ladies with white gloves and fancy hats. They were real women, hurt women, women who were doing their best to live out their faith. They came and gave me flowers, food, and a part of themselves. They showed me that compassion was not a noun but an action word. And when they left, I no longer felt flat. My heart was too full for that."

Sharing Stories, Sharing Lives

Healing occurs not only in receiving friendship and kindness, but also in giving it. In the context of writing together and sharing your stories, you have the opportunity to do both. In my groups, as different members have struggled with metastatic cancer, a solid community of support has quickly formed. We have written to our colleagues in the hospital or visited and kept a bedside vigil as they've gone into comas. We have even created memorial booklets for the family, containing the stories and poems of the deceased group member. Stories are a powerful legacy. "The writing group," a daughter of a former writing group member said, "kept my mother going all these many weeks." The act of offering support and affection in the final days of a fellow writer's life not only allows group members to express their affection, but it brings them even closer to one another and helps everyone to confront their own fears and sorrow.

"It has all been wonderful," Karen wrote. "Writing in a group as friendships grow, forming bonds, sharing sorrows and laughter, has been invaluable." Judy agreed. "There is a wonderful strength in fighting a common enemy.... It is like warm and affirming friends who truly understand." Clarissa added, "Writing with the other women who are undergoing the same journey is liberating. The feelings just flow out, and you don't edit your emotions. It gave me an excuse to be human. There are lots of others like me."

EXERCISE 2: COLLABORATIVE POEM MAKING

By this session, you'll find that the bonds between the group members have strengthened and that a warmth and easy rapport now exists. The writing will be strong and beautiful, and you will hear at least as much laughter as weeping. A buzz of conversation dominates the breaks, along with offers of help and support to those who may be undergoing another series of treatments, tests, or surgeries.

This group exercise in poem making honors the shared experience of cancer in a different way than the other exercises have done thus far. Everyone is sure to enjoy the activity of creating a poem together. This exercise also allows those who might not otherwise try it to ease into poem making in a less threatening way.

There are many ways to create collaborative poems. Here's one approach that I have used successfully with my groups. To begin, you'll need several sheets of colored paper, each with a different word one it. The words should be associated with the cancer experience, for example, *diagnosis, surgery, radiation, chemotherapy, fear,* and *scar.* (Depending on the size of your group, you might need two identical sets of sheets, using as many as six or seven different cancer-related words).

Give each person a sheet of colored paper and invite the group to write one line describing an image or feeling the key word evokes. For example, an image of getting radiation might be described with these words: "I am frozen; embraced by the white cast, I hold my breath."

Take only one or two minutes for each line. Poetry allows us to see the world with new eyes and opens us to our emotions quickly. For this exercise, suggest that the participants merely aim for "first thought, best thought." In this exercise, encourage spontaneity over deliberation, freshness and risk taking over correctness.

Once each person has written her description, everyone passes their paper to the right, writes a description of the next word, and so on, until everyone has written once or twice on each sheet of paper.

Split the large group into smaller groups of four to six people. Divide the colored sheets equally among the groups. Offer scissors and tape, instructing them to "play" with the lines they have been given, looking for images that connect and build on each other. Encourage them to rearrange the lines any way they wish to create their poem. Allow thirty minutes for this exercise. Unlike other writing exercises, this is a noisy one. You'll hear the buzz of voices, discussion, and laughter as the strips of colored paper are moved around. When the time is up, reconvene the full group and read each of the group poems aloud, inviting responses from their listeners.

Here are two excerpts from some collaborative poems completed in small groups of four people each:

SCAR
My scar is my private badge of courage,
pinkish nubby river across my chest
Floating skin that rises and falls
... a willow branch.

DIAGNOSIS
Sucks.
I am not a diagnosis.
I am not my diagnosis.
My diagnosis is not me.
Diagnosis is not a judgment.
One person's opinion;
Hard to hear.
No Thank You.

This exercise, which engages everyone in the shared attempt to create a poem, always generates excitement and fun. It also provides an opportunity for group members to discuss what makes the poem work best: why some images are retained and others discarded, how what emerges expresses the uniqueness and yet the universal aspects of the cancer experience. There is also the simple pleasure of engaging with poem making in a physical way: cutting and rearranging, taping, and combining disparate parts into a whole. "Gosh," one participant eagerly remarked as she took the scissors and began cutting the colored papers into strips, "this is like being back in grade school! This is fun!"

A Closing Poem: Let Evening Come

Two years ago, I attended a session at the National Poetry Therapy conference led by the poets Caryn Mirriam-Goldberg and Perie Longo, who are also practicing poetry therapists. Caryn introduced Jane Kenyon's poem "Let Evening Come," using it as a closing circle activity, and I have incorporated it into my groups ever since. The repetition of the phrase "let evening come" has a chanting quality reminiscent of the healing songs of the Native Americans:

Let the fox go back to its sandy den.
Let the wind die down. Let the shed
go black inside. Let evening come.

To the bottle in the ditch, to the scoop
in the oats, to air in the lung
let evening come.

Let it come, as it will, and don't
be afraid. God does not leave us
comfortless, so let evening come.

Read the poem together, with each person reading one line until you reach the end. Now read it again aloud in its entirety. As you form the closing circle, ask each person to offer one thing for which they are grateful or for which they hope or pray, followed with the line "let evening come." Do this until everyone has spoken. Close the session with your own words of gratitude and adjourn, saying, "Let evening come."

Suggested Format for Session Six

GUIDED VISUALIZATION: THE CIRCLE OF FRIENDS

The meditation is followed by five minutes of writing that describes the healing circle of friends. Invite the circle to read aloud without response.

EXERCISE 1: HELPING HANDS

Pass around a photograph of helping hands or hands clasped in friendship. Think about times when you have experienced unexpected friendship or support during your cancer journey. Write for fifteen minutes, followed by reading and two or three responses per reader.

SHORT BREAK *(ten minutes)*

EXERCISE 2: COLLABORATIVE POEM MAKING

Using sheets of colored paper with one cancer word written at the top, each participant writes one line that describes an image she associates with the word or her feelings about it. Pass the sheets to the right until everyone has written a descriptive phrase on each. Divide the large group into smaller groups of four to six, distributing the colored sheets equally between each group. Provide each group with scissors and tape. Allow thirty minutes for the poem making, followed by reconvening as a whole group and sharing the poems aloud.

CLOSING POEM: "LET EVENING COME" BY JANE KENYON

First, read Kenyon's poem aloud as a group, with each person saying one line until you reach the end. Then read the poem aloud once more. In your closing circle, ask each person to offer one gratitude, hope, or prayer, followed with the phrase "let evening come." Close the session by saying, "Let evening come."

CHAPTER SEVEN

FAITH AND SPIRITUALITY

*Perhaps it is not so much for us to find meaning in life
as to give meaning to what life brings us.*

—VICTOR FRANKL, *Man's Search for Meaning*

Guided Visualization: What Matters Now?

Sit comfortably in your seat, and relax by taking a few deep breaths. Close your eyes or soft-focus on a spot in front of you. Let your breathing gradually become deeper and fuller, noticing, as you inhale and exhale, how you bring in oxygen to fill your lungs and blood vessels with fresh energy, fueling your body and mind. As you exhale, feel the tensions you've carried all day subside. Let your body and mind relax: your body softening and settling, your thoughts becoming freer. See the images floating before your eyes, one after the other. Feel the natural rhythm of your breathing, letting it lull you into a space of calm and quiet. As you become more relaxed, return to the healing place where you've traveled before: a peaceful place, full of beauty; a place that knows you, and that you know deeply; a place where you feel nurtured; a place of healing. Today, you come with questions about your life. Perhaps you want to invite someone, your wise person or inner healer, to join you as you travel back over time, over your life, to those moments that made a difference, shaping all you are, informing all you have become. Be aware of what comes to mind, the images and feelings of each image. Linger over those memories that seem especially powerful or important to you. Ask your wise person to help you make sense of each event: why it mattered, what hopes you had, and what you learned from each. What, during your whole life, have you have carried with you to help you through difficult times? What have you learned that can be helpful or healing to you now? Ask your wise person to guide you, to look ahead to the life in front of you, the one you have now. Ask, "What matters now?" Listen as your wise person speaks to you, and quietly receive the wisdom that is offered. Slowly, make your way back into the outer world. When you are ready, open your eyes and begin writing. You might start with the line "what matters now is . . ." Write for five minutes.

Faith and Spirituality During Cancer

Your experiences with cancer are influenced by your religious or spiritual beliefs—the meaning they hold for you, how you feel about your illness, and how well you cope. Faith and spirituality, whether or not they are expressed through organized religion, are important aspects of our lives, and during difficult and stressful times, they can provide strength and comfort. "This [spirituality] was the most important aspect of the whole process," Irena, a writing group member, said.

Kristen confessed that she had never gone to church regularly, but during her treatment felt the need to go to a church and feel something bigger than herself. "I think I needed a boost in the power of faith," she said. "Faith, I have decided, is an important part of the human life."

Everyone has a spiritual dimension. We can experience spiritual moments at any time: when we are close to nature, with a loved one, hearing a beautiful symphony, seeing a great work of art, helping someone in need, or entering a house of worship and sensing a greater power.

A life-threatening disease like cancer presents you with a new set of realities and questions. You may find you turn more frequently to your spiritual beliefs for strength and comfort. When you live with cancer, it's quite common to want to understand what having cancer means to you. In fact, cancer may cause you to look at life in new ways. You may reflect on the purpose of your life and what you value most. "An awareness of a higher power is part of the cancer experience," Nancy said. "The joy of . . . being grateful for each and every day is an integral part of the experience. You respect the very fine line between life and death. Your awareness is honed. . . . You live in the present."

On the other hand, serious illness can affect your spiritual outlook. You may feel angry and question your faith. "I do feel this challenged my faith," Genel wrote. Even if you ultimately emerge, as Genel did, with a stronger faith, you may struggle to understand why cancer entered your life, asking, "Why me?"

When cancer strikes, you might even feel abandoned by God or a higher power. "I haven't felt closer to God during this experience," Laura said. "If anything, I've felt less close to God lately. I'm still feeling the pain of the shock of getting cancer, and I know I feel angry about it."

Cancer as a Turning Point

Whatever your spiritual or religious beliefs, cancer gives you opportunities as well as challenges to redefine yourself, your world, and your relationship to life. "As part of our wholeness," Stephen Levine remarked in a 1994 interview with *The Sun,* "we need our woundedness. It seems written into spirituality that there's a dark side to which we much expose ourselves." Cancer may provoke a dark night of the soul, but it may also allow you to deepen your self-understanding and your compassion for others.

Nancy, who traveled to Thailand after she recovered, attributed some of her redefinition to her experience of observing the Thais, of how, as Buddhists, they took strength from their beliefs in dealing with the devastation of the 2004 tsunami: "Any particular life is one of the many ways to nirvana," she said in a speech to breast cancer survivors at the Northern California Cancer Center's 2005 conference. "This allows them to mourn but move on . . . suddenly I was very bored with cancer. I no longer let it define me."

Research has shown that having a strong spiritual belief system can be very beneficial to our health and well-being. Dr. Larry Dossey, in his eloquent and thoughtful book on prayer and health, *Healing Words: The Power of Prayer and the Practice of Medicine,* summarized some of the key research on prayer and healing, starting with the first study in 1872 by Sir Francis Galton. A number of studies since have demonstrated the positive influences of prayer on health and healing among a variety of patients, including those with breast cancer, HIV, and coronary disease. "My faith grew and deepened. I prayed a lot," Nancy said. Judy agreed. "I'm a Catholic, and I did pray. I got a blessing for the sick from the priest."

Charlene expressed surprise as she learned, once again, how to pray during cancer. "I felt uncomfortable with the frequent offers and requests for prayers," she said, but as her treatment progressed, she felt overwhelmed and turned to prayer, acknowledging the comforting familiarity of her early Christian background. Paula affirmed the power of prayer in helping her own healing process. "I believe that everyone's prayers helped me make it through with grace and strength," she said.

There are many forms of prayer, including those of thanksgiving, praise, or help. Prayers are found in every religion and culture and written in every language. They have been described as expressions of love. Jean Shinoda Bolen describes them as healing words. Healing touch is yet another form of prayer. Using imagery, Dr. Martin Rossman tells us, is also like prayer. We enter into an inner dialogue, not with a higher being, but with our own higher consciousness.

Writing, poet Denise Levertov once said, is a form of prayer. It is deeply meditative, and as we write regularly, our awareness is deepened. Writer Julia Cameron also describes writing as a powerful form of prayer and meditation, one that can connect us to our insights and to a deeper level of inner guidance. Writing can lead us into prayer, even becoming the prayer itself. It allows us to let healing in.

Writing through cancer can be one kind of prayer—an appeal to God or a higher power, an exploration of faith, a deep soul-searching, or a way to give thanks to God. This kind of prayer enables us to keep perspective, a crucial way to create an environment in which spiritual transformation can take place. During the cancer journey, writing as a form of prayer can be an especially deeply meditative and spiritual activity. "The community I am building with my fellow writers and other who have had cancer is, in a sense, a form of spirituality," Laura said. Through writing, we embark on a deep inner journey where we discover the meaning of our lives, the importance of other people, the ways in which cancer has changed us forever. We also confront our own mortality as never before. In these ways, writing can be deeply spiritual and transformational.

EXERCISE 1: THE FLOW OF LIFE

In this exercise, you are invited to reflect on the larger forces of life and on your faith and spirituality. In Buddhism, understanding nourishes faith, and the act of looking deeply within ourselves not only fosters self-understanding, but it also can strengthen our faith. Illness can be a catalyst to personal transformation. Spirituality is, in many respects, the awareness of something bigger than us, a life force beyond our own humanity. "All things are connected," Chief Seattle of the Squamish tribe is to have said. The Zen master Isutsu wrote that "the very act of the artist expressing his interior is in itself nothing other that the act of Nature expressing its own interior."

You can begin this exercise in multiple ways. One way is by making two lists: one of positive life events and the other of times of hardship. Sometimes I ask individuals to draw a simple life line, from birth to the present, dividing it into decades and quickly marking the high points in their lives as well as the struggles or challenges.

What quickly emerges is a visual pattern of ebb and flow, ups and downs, joys and sorrows as part of the life journey. Examine your lifeline and think about life cycles, those you observe in your own life and in the natural world. Reflect on those times of hardship and what helped you deal with each one. Write for twenty minutes.

This exercise stimulates many different responses from participants. Ceci wrote a piece she titled "You Can't Push the River," in which she imagined herself as a drop of water in the stream of life: "I'm only one droplet flowing into one of countless rivers that ultimately join the oceans of God.... How dare I fight against this force? Yet, somehow I still do, even knowing that my destiny is clear. I guess it's all about the journey, the struggle, the ultimate reward."

Laura, who was still in the midst of chemotherapy treatments and was struggling with her faith, wrote a poem that expressed her pain, and ultimately, her surrender to a higher power:

I lay there, miserable and wretched ...
Lord have mercy ...

A wad of pain
in the pit of my stomach
Lord have mercy

I focus on it
Lord have mercy
Lord have mercy
Lord have mercy ...

The wad unwinds
Lord have mercy

The wondering stops
Lord have mercy

Suffering stops
Lord have mercy

I lay there peacefully
Lord have mercy
And he does ...

Varda, who ultimately lost her life to metastasized cancer, wrote about the role faith played in her life before and after cancer:

God and I always had a special relationship, sealed in ancient Hebrew prayers and stained-glass windows. The Shofar blown on Yom Kippur. The Book of Life open for ten days a year, and then my fate sealed.

But our relationship has changed. In asking me to surrender to this illness, God has asked me to let go—to trust—float free. And I have found this to be a most precious time.

My cancer has challenged my faith, and I have found an incredible well I did not know I had. I have found true surrender, enormous peace.

EXERCISE 2: GRATITUDE

In the midst of illness or suffering, it often helps to be reminded of the things that give us joy or comfort, that make us laugh or feel nourished; it can be valuable to remember the gifts of friendship and love that help us heal. For this exercise, you'll need one small gift-wrapped box. You might use photographs or poetry, such as those in Connie Zucker Reider's photographic essay, *In Shadow and Light: Looking for the Gifts of Cancer,* or the poem "Gifts" by Patti Marshock, from *The Cancer Poetry Project,* as accompaniments to this exercise.

Reider, a photographer and breast cancer survivor, charts her own journey through a collection of beautiful photographic images and accompanying text. Marshock, an oncology nurse, describes how patients often give her little gifts to show their appreciation for her work. Yet she describes the real gifts as the patients' strength and courage she witnesses every day, beautifully described in her poem "Gifts." Here is an excerpt:

She gives you a present, a little doll, handmade
of empty spools and new buttons, held together with floral wire.
It looks like you: your brown hair, brown eyes,
In a uniform just the color of yours,
Wearing a tinsel halo. You look at her fading frame and
Wonder why she used her precious time in such a way.

Using the small gift box as inspiration, think about the many gifts you have received during your cancer experience: offerings of friendship, small gestures of kindness, anything that made a difference to you. For twenty minutes, write about any of these gifts and your gratitude for them. Lillian wrote about her gratitude for the many gifts her cancer experience had given her: "The gifts of compassion: I feel more able to reach out to others in pain and suffering to a degree I only imaged before cancer.... The gift of accompanying my brother during his final days with us, final breath, last sound and touch. Gifts and gratefulness." Judy wrote about the new appreciation for life that she now had: "Each new day is a gift for which I am grateful. I treasure the simple pleasures that life has to offer."

Candice, in a short piece entitled "Thank You," wrote about the gifts of her cancer writing group: "We are a community of women ... and survivors of cancer.... A community of women whose poetry drips from their pens like iridescent drops of dew, whose stories excite, sadden, entertain, filling in the voids left by disease and death. I thank each one of you."

Our spiritual journeys are intimately bound to our psychological and emotional journeys. Compassion, self-love, deepening, and awakening are all parts of the spiritual paths we travel when we write truthfully from our hearts. Writing through cancer, as Carolyn, a writing group member, so eloquently described, "becomes your prayer book, your daily office, and like a monk, you faithfully mark the liturgical hours of your involuntary vocation with the canticles and sacred texts of the cancer library."

Writing and giving voice to your spiritual journey helps you to confront yourself, to open your heart to caring, love, and connectedness with one another. This process is at the heart of spirituality and of healing.

A Closing Poem: The Navajo Night Chant

Several years ago, I came across a short Navajo prayer that has its origins in the sacred rituals of healing songs and chants. I now regularly use it in my writing groups.

For the Navajo, chanting is a celebration of life, harmony, and healing. The Navajo Night Chant is an important example of the interrelatedness of language, healing, and spirituality. Here are some lines:

Happily I recover.
Happily my interior becomes cool.
Happily I go forth.
My interior feeling cool, may I walk.
No longer sore, may I walk.
Impervious to pain, may I walk . . .

Happily may I walk.
Being as it used to be long ago, may I walk.
May it be beautiful before me,
May it be beautiful behind me,
May it be beautiful below me,
May it be beautiful above me,
May it be beautiful all around me.
In beauty it is finished.

If you are writing as part of a group, first read the entire Night Chant aloud. As you form your closing circle, have each person read one line aloud as you move around the circle. A beautiful way to close the session is to have each participant offer one line, for example, "may it be beautiful before *you*," as a blessing to the person next to her, until everyone has offered and received a blessing. Close the session with the last line "In beauty it is finished."

Suggested Format for Session Seven

GUIDED VISUALIZATION: WHAT MATTERS NOW?

The meditation is followed by five minutes of writing. Invite the circle to read aloud without response. As a prelude, I sometimes place a copy of Margaret Robison's poem "What Matters Then?" from her book Red Creek, a Requiem on each participant's chair before the session begins.

EXERCISE 1: THE FLOW OF LIFE

Pass around a rough, jagged stone, comparing its sharp edges to the way grief, a cancer diagnosis, or another traumatic life event often feels. Follow it with a small basket of smooth, river stones, letting each person select one as a symbol of how raw emotions are softened and smoothed over time, allowing you to find the strength to heal. Consider your own life journeys and what has given you strength in times of hardship.
Write for twenty minutes.

SHORT BREAK *(ten minutes)*

EXERCISE 2: GRATITUDE

Place a small gift-wrapped box in the center of the circle. Discuss how gifts come to us in small, sometimes unexpected ways. Think about the times during your cancer experience when you were given a gift of some kind or when you felt gratitude. For twenty minutes, write about gifts or gratitude.

CLOSING POEM: "THE NAVAJO NIGHT CHANT"

Everyone will need a copy of the chant. Talk about the tradition of healing chants among Native Americans. Read the Night Chant aloud to the group. Form a circle, and using the passage that begins "May it be beautiful before me," ask each person to offer a blessing to the person on her right, substituting the word you in place of me until everyone has had a turn. Close the session with the last line, "In beauty, it is finished."

CHAPTER EIGHT

RECURRENCE AND DEATH

You must grieve for this right now
—you have to feel this sorrow now—
for the world must be loved this much
if you're going to say "I lived."

—NAZIM HIKMET, "On Living," from *Poems of Nazim Hikmet*

Guided Visualization: From Darkness into Light

Settle comfortably in your seat and begin by taking a few deep, relaxing breaths, in and out, in and out. As you breathe in, be aware of your lungs filling with fresh oxygen that fuels your body and mind. As you breathe out, let go of any remaining stresses or tensions from the day, anything that takes you away from simply being here, in this room, in this quiet place. Feel the gentle warmth and support from each other, knowing that you are held in safety and love. Now imagine that you are traveling through a long tunnel, surrounded by darkness and embraced by shadows. If you begin to feel tense or anxious, look ahead, far off in the distance, and you will see the warm glow of a light at the end of the dark tunnel. Take solace in knowing that, despite the journey into darkness, there will always be light beckoning you on, but first, you must travel through the darkness and your fears. As you move through the tunnel, notice the darkness. Let your eyes become accustomed to it, paying attention to what you feel as you make your way through the blackness. Perhaps your body tenses up, or perhaps you are afraid of what might lurk in the shadows. Allow yourself to look into those shadows. See what it is that you fear. Look at it directly. Speak to it. Acknowledge it. If you feel anxious or threatened, look toward the light at the tunnel's end and feel it, sensing the warmth and safety that beckons you on through the darkness. Once you arrive in the light, take a few moments to look back at the tunnel and to celebrate your courage. Slowly begin to return to this room, this place of warmth and safety. When you are ready, take five minutes to write about your journey into the darkness.

The Fear of Recurrence

During the cancer journey, the fear lurking in your heart and mind is usually tied to recurrence, or even death. "Fears of recurrence are very common," says oncologist Marisa Weiss, founder of Breastcancer.org and coauthor of *Living Beyond Breast Cancer.* "They're particularly persistent as you're first leaving active treatment. You may expect that you'll want to throw yourself a party on your last day of chemo or radiation, only to find that you're a little melancholy or fearful, thinking, 'Maybe I should be getting more treatments just to be sure?'"

"Treatments keep you busy and occupied, and they take a long time," New York film critic and cancer survivor Jamie Bernard wrote in *Breast Cancer There and Back: A Woman-to-Woman Guide.* "When you finish treatment you're at loose ends, wondering if [the cancer] will come back. I was having six-month checkups, and then my oncologist said, 'I'll see you in a year.' I said, 'What? Are you sure you don't want to see me before then?' I told him I'd start camping out in the hall waiting for appointments. You want to think that someone's still watching."

Anyone who has had cancer has lived with the possibility of a recurrence. Even though being cancer-free for five years is thought to signal full recovery, recurrence can occur many years after the first diagnosis. One of my friends lived cancer-free for nine years after treatment for ovarian cancer. Then a malignant lump in her neck was discovered, and the following year, cancer appeared in her breast. "Recurrence is always there as a possibility," Irena, a writing group member wrote. It "is like a betrayal by the body, and once it happens, it can happen again."

Recurrence, even though it is not always synonymous with a death sentence, is that dark possibility you push as far from your mind as possible.

In a 2001 study of the breast cancer survivor's fears of recurrence, researchers found that the most common fears revolved around the possibility of death, further treatment, emotional difficulties, pain, advancement of the disease, suffering of family members, and loss of a breast. Survivors' fears were triggered by such things as thinking about the future after cancer; annual checkups, where recurrence could be diagnosed; physical reminders of cancer; and being around others with cancer. Just ten months after her own diagnosis of cancer, one writer's mother died from inflammatory breast cancer, prompting her to finally seek professional help to deal with her own fears of recurrence and death.

Charlene described how although she thought she was losing her fearfulness she discovered that her first follow-up mammogram triggered it all over again: "Within minutes I reverted to the cold panic of a first diagnosis," she wrote. "The results were inconclusive, and I had to wait three months ... until the baseline could be compared with the result.... If anything medical puts me into a state of uncertainty, recurrence encroaches my perimeter, breathing a cold reminder of my own raw fear."

Genel echoed what many others describe: "Recurrence is what I fear most," she said. "[With] every little ache or pain or swelling, I freeze.... Rationally I know I just have to live each day and pray that there will be no recurrence. I have thought about death a lot in the last couple of years, due to my husband's ... death and my experience with cancer. Mostly I fear it because I want to spend more time with my children."

EXERCISE 1: THE QUESTIONS IN YOUR MIND

As you first return to a life not defined by surgeries, radiation appointments, or a regimen of chemotherapy, questions about or fear of recurrence and the future may weigh heavily on your mind. This is a tender time, and giving voice to those deepest fears can create some poignant and deeply intimate writing. One prompt that often helps these fears to surface in my writing groups is the poem "Questions in the Mind of the Poet as She Washes the Floors," in *Mercy, Mercy Me,* by Elena Georgiou. Here is an excerpt:

Is it enough for me to know where I'm from?

If I do more truth-telling will I be happier with what I say?
If I had three days to live would I still be sensible?

Is the break between my feelings and my memory
the reason I'm unable to sustain rage?

Am I a peninsula slowly turning into an island?

If a surgeon cut out my mistakes
would the scar be under my heart?

Each stanza is a question the poet asks, so if you are writing as a group, first read the poem aloud together, with each person reading one of the poet's questions. As you read the poem a second time, underline the one question that you find most compelling. As a group, you can even read aloud together a third time, creating a "new" poem, by having each person read the one question she has underlined. Notice how the poem changes. Using the question you've underlined as your prompt, or asking a question of your own, write for twenty minutes. Reflect on what emerges in your writing.

Sheree chose the line "If I can see a cup drop to the floor and shatter why can't I see it gather itself back together?" and wrote a short piece entitled "Just in Case":

JUST IN CASE

If I can see a cup drop to the floor and shatter, why can't I see it gather itself back together?

Sometimes, mostly in the middle of the night, I tell my husband that I'm scared. He asks me why. He tells me that I need to think more positively.

I'm not trying to think negatively, but the images that come to mind at the oddest of times frighten me. A funeral, friends saying nice things about me, my youngest daughter's tears.

Then I force an about-face, I imagine my white blood cells charging at the abnormal cells. I don't know if there are any abnormal cells left, but I have to imagine it anyway, just in case.

I'm doing a lot of things now, just in case.

Another writer, who was struggling with a second diagnosis of cancer, directed her questions directly to the disease:

Why are you back? I know this is a test for me, an eye-opener, another wake-up call, an encouragement, maybe even a gift. I can't really figure it out yet....

Should I fear you, fear death? Absolutely. Can we coexist? I suppose. Can I surpass, get the upper hand, come back again? We'll see....

Do I thank you or fear you; embrace you or just hold on for now?

Judy had also experienced a recurrence, and in response to Georgiou's poem, she asked, "Can I Be Happy with the Person I've Become?":

I found a lump ten years ago, underwent a lumpectomy
and radiation, and survived, passed the test with flying colors.

I thought I was home free, safe, and went on with life.
I was optimistic ...

Then cancer struck again ...
I felt betrayed, no longer sure of the future ...

In a piece entitled "Recurrence," Laura described her feelings when someone she loved was affected by a second diagnosis of cancer:

Before her cancer returned, we were just getting to know one another,
sitting side by side in the sand,
staring out at the sea from which we'd emerged,
bruised and dripping, a while before.
I wave to her now,
hope she can hear the song I sing to her.
Wishing so much that she will join me on shore again.

Carol wrote a poem entitled "Afraid" in an attempt to describe her own fears of recurrence and death:

I wake this morning
stomach tight again,
afraid, again,
same dreams, struggling
out of breath . . .

She quells her anxiety by remembering to breathe and to notice the small gifts of being alive:

I breathe in the moments,
This is all I have.

Facing Death

Although a diagnosis of cancer is not a death sentence, it does bring us face-to-face with our own mortality. Fear of death and recurrence lies just beneath the surface. When you write about your cancer experience, you have a rich opportunity to confront the relationship between it and your fear of death, learning from it and about yourself.

Mary Jo, who has been fighting a rare form of bone cancer for many years, wrote poignantly of her struggle with her disease and of her will to overcome death:

As water threatens to engulf me
I dig deeper within
looking for the strength to resurface.
The downward force continues
            Uninterrupted
            Interminable.

My body and mind are so exhausted from the struggle
that turning my will over to the force
appears to offer comfort.

But that is only an illusion.
Just as I am losing the battle
my spirit, battered, but still fighting,
speaks to me.

Joan, recovering from surgery for kidney cancer, used the setting of an inner city card game to take us directly into the fears associated with cancer. Entitled "Wild Card," her piece begins:

They perch on their haunches on the stoop, on the mean streets of the Inner City: the boys dealing cards. Shuffle, trump, rap a little; build a fire in an old barrel; wear gloves with no fingers, and at dusk everyone but The Boys scurries off like roaches, leaving the gamblers behind and you only ever saw it in the movies till now.

Then the narrator suddenly realizes she's playing the game:

You gambled all your life you know, you get it now. The Dealer holds the cards, you read the cards you're dealt. Discard a few just like the Corner Boys have done, just like you imagined them to do and here you are with your own hand to play.

Finally, in a chilling climax, we hear the terror as she confronts her reality:

Hit me.
Two cards down. Two more dealt and one is this New Love Of Your Life and one of course, The Wild One, is your get outta' jail free card, your wild card, the cancer card . . . the wild card stark in your hand . . . the cancer card.
Suddenly you don't wanna' play.
You want your discard back, you want to fold . . . you were so certain that you didn't belong in this neighborhood here playing cards, but
Oh-Yes-You-Do.

In an interview with Derrick Jensen for *The Sun,* Marc Barasch, a Buddhist healer, reminds us that "any exploration of our relationship with disease—and in fact, our relationship with life—has to start with the understanding that we are going to die, that we are vulnerable. . . . Once we have accepted this as our starting point, then we can move toward another realization that goes hand in hand with the first: that death, as well as being our companion for life, is also a fundamental spiritual metaphor and a fundamental spiritual experience."

"When I was forced to accept death as a fact of my life—and perhaps one that I would face sooner rather than later," Kathy LaTour wrote in her book *The Breast Cancer Companion,* "I finally had the big picture about my cancer. I could look at the past and the future and know that there were no guarantees, but that I could make decisions about what I could control. From that came an indescribable peace."

When we examine the root meaning of the word *healing,* we find that it implies that we become whole in body, mind, and spirit. It does not, Barasch reminds us, mean that we are free of cancer. "We can be both ill *and* healed— whole within our affliction." Confronting your fear of death and exploring the ways it can inform your life is a deeply human journey. Yet it is difficult territory to travel as you write. How do you help one another confront your deepest fears? When I lead my own groups, more often than not, it is the loss of a member that brings everyone's fears into the open.

When a Group Member Dies

Writing together is often a journey through treatment, recovery, and the return to a normal life. The shared journey from diagnosis through recovery is always a reminder to everyone of how precious life is. But not everyone will survive. When a group member dies, you not only experience loss, but you may also find that your own fears are rekindled. You will want to find ways to honor the life of a lost fellow writer, while allowing each other the chance to grieve and to face your own fear of death.

How do you deal with the issue of death in a writing group for people with cancer? The loss of a fellow writer or friend to cancer provokes grieving, sorrow, and fear. Judy, who experienced the death of two members during her participation in a writing group said, "One of the hardest things is watching other women get sick and die. I wasn't ready to hear someone I'd been writing with was gone. How would I continue, knowing someone else would get sick and die? It brings my own mortality closer. It is the part of me that is holding my breath."

In the PBS series *Healing and the Mind,* Bill Moyers spoke with Dr. David Spiegel of Stanford Hospital about the impact of a member's death on Spiegel's therapeutic cancer support groups. Spiegel remarked, "No doubt one part of what they were feeling was, "There but for the grace of God go I.'"

Irena's prognosis was favorable; nonetheless, she shared, "[I was] very aware of my mortality, and I lived for a while in the fear of dying way too young." Her greater fear was of losing a friend or loved one to cancer. When her dear friend Varda died from metastatic breast cancer, Irena said, "Losing Varda was the most difficult, not because I was afraid, but because the cancer took her brain, sanity, and presence before she died."

When I first experienced the loss of a writing group member to cancer, it was an opportunity for me to learn from her death. A physician with metastatic breast cancer, she attended my pilot program, knowing from the outset that she had only a few months left to live. She spoke candidly about her illness and prognosis, yet, as the leader, I was timid and tiptoed around the issue of death.

As the pilot ended, she told me how important the writing group had been to her in the last months of life. But she also had some advice and counseled me not to be afraid to help the group confront their fears of mortality. "Every one of us who has cancer needs to acknowledge those fears," she said.

From that point on, I incorporated exercises that offered the opportunity to write about recurrence and death. I discovered that in doing so, I grew as a leader, and the group members developed even stronger bonds with each other. Now, whenever anyone in my writing groups faces a terminal diagnosis, a strong circle of help and support is quick to form. Our shared experience is truly enriched as we share in the final weeks of a fellow writer's life.

"We are like a family now," Judy said after the death of a friend and fellow writer. "We know each other's heart and soul, what makes us laugh and cry. . . . It is terrifying when it is someone you really love, but because of the writing experience, I had a secret knowledge and could hold her closer because of it."

ALTERNATE EXERCISE: A RITUAL OF REMEMBRANCE

When family members or friends die, you often hear people remark that they wish they could have had one more chance to tell them they were loved or would be missed. "I have lost two friends from accidents," Judy said. "At least with cancer you have time to say good-bye to the people you love."

When a group member is dying, it is important to take the opportunity to tell her how much she is loved or will be missed. Here is an optional exercise that I've found to be helpful in the process of grieving together and honoring the life of a fellow writer.

In a group, this will likely be an emotional session, but it is an important one, for it reminds you that in any group in which the experience of a life-threatening illness is shared, you need rituals to honor the lives and memories of those whom you lose, get your grief and feelings into the open, and create the safety to express your fears.

Rituals lend significance to life passages. They help you find ways to express what you feel, especially when someone's life is ending. The rituals that have become part of your regular writing group will become even more important at times of loss and grief, ensuring the safety and comfort of mourning together.

Grieving together carries its own reassurance: you are not alone in this struggle. Sharing a member's death creates much more closeness between group members. Sharing grieving affirms your lives. In the Moyers interview, Spiegel observed that grieving together gives "a message to us that when our time comes, we will not slip away unnoticed, but that we will be grieved and cared about and missed. Seeing that what we do is appreciated and cherished by the people we care about makes dying less frightening than it otherwise would be."

This exercise focuses on the person being remembered. With the group, spend a short time honoring the dying member. You might begin by lighting a candle in the center of your circle, inviting a few moments of silence in respect for her. Then invite each person to tell their fondest remembrances of their colleague and her writing. Honor the silences between each person's words, giving everyone the time to speak, if they feel moved to do so. Be sure to have boxes of tissues handy.

When you have completed your spoken remembrances, offer each group member a blank sheet of stationery—paper chosen especially for this occasion. Invite them to write a letter to the person or, if she has already died, a letter of remembrance for the remaining family members. It is good to allow ample time for this exercise, perhaps as long as a half hour. If you choose to do it, read aloud without response.

Once you have finished reading, offer a song, a prayer, or a poem to mark the end of your ritual. I have used a modification of the "Navajo Night Chant" introduced in chapter 7. Each person speaks her blessing to the one being honored, saying for example, "May it be beautiful all around her." When it is your turn, conclude with "In beauty, it is finished." Collect the completed letters and bind them in a booklet that can then be taken or sent to the dying person and her family.

The legacy of a person's life can be honored and affirmed by the poems and stories she leaves behind—one of the most powerful gifts of the writing group to family and friends. They give family and friends a powerful remembrance of a loved one's life fully lived. In my writing groups, stories or poems written by a deceased group member—those they have given permission to share—have been an integral part of the memorial services, with sons, daughters, and friends reading the loved one's writing. We have created booklets and circulated them to relatives and close friends as a remembrance. When the husband of a deceased group member received the booklet of his wife's writing, he called to thank me, overcome with emotion, yet deeply grateful. "I couldn't put it down," he said. "You have no idea what it means to my children and me." The power of writing to heal our wounded spirits goes well beyond the journey of the person whose life is lost to cancer. A loved one's writing can also help in healing the sorrow of her grieving family and friends.

EXERCISE 2: HOW I WANT TO BE REMEMBERED

Cancer, regardless of type or stage, foists on you a certain awareness of your mortality as you go through treatments. Sharing in the experience of a group member's death also gives you pause for reflection on your life. "As people face death," Marcia wrote, "it forces us to write about what we, too, are afraid of: to look death in the face. It is wonderful to be able to bring it into the open, let it be examined and felt so deeply." Marcia was inspired to write about death in a short poem entitled "Mortality." In it, she asks a question of the reader:

What would you do differently
if you knew you only had
the rest of your life to live?

Janice, suffering from metastatic breast cancer, also reflected on the issue of mortality: "Why is it that only facing our mortality spurs us on to action? Why can't we live every day as if it were our last? Think of how differently we would act. . . . Every day is a renewed chance to start over. . . . Every day my children and I build new memories. The memories will survive, even after I'm gone."

What would you do differently? What memories do you want to leave behind? When your time comes, how do you want to be remembered? Marilyn Nelson's poem "Cover Photograph," from *The Fields of Praise*, provides the inspiration for a writing exercise that prompts you to think about how you'd like to be remembered:

I want to be remembered
with a dark face absorbing all colors
and giving them back twice as brightly,
like water remembering light.

I want to be remembered
with a simple name, like Mama:
as an open door from creation,
as a picture of someone you know.

When leading a writing group, I like to accompany Nelson's poem with a number of magazines, all with women pictured on the covers. As you look at the cover photographs, write down the adjectives or images that come to mind. If some of the photos are of famous women, list examples of what you'll remember about each. (It's useful to also have some images of women whose reputations might not evoke the most positive remembrances, as well as some of those who are known for their outstanding accomplishments!)

After you've reacted to the photographs, you can initiate a group reading of Marilyn Nelson's poem, with each person taking a stanza. Now, imagining that your picture is on a magazine cover at the time of your death, answer the question, "How do I want to be remembered?" and write for twenty minutes. Carol, experiencing a recurrence of breast cancer, began by writing in first person, saying, "I want to be remembered as a loving family member and true friend." Midway, she shifted to third person, writing as if she was being remembered by others: "Carol has grown from learning to live on her own ... learning from her bouts with the first and second cancers she endured.... Carol loved people and loved life to the fullest. She will be in each of our hearts forever."

Another writer, who wished to remain anonymous, wrote: "I want to be remembered as someone who found a way to forgive, as someone who learned to leave anger behind and embrace an imperfect world. I want to be remembered as someone who found her way home through illness and suffering, a prodigal daughter forgiven and forgiving."

A Closing Poem: I Will Not Die an Unlived Life

More than twenty years ago, educator Dawna Markova was diagnosed with leukemia. In her book *I Will Not Die an Unlived Life: Reclaiming Passion and Purpose,* she offers us a poem that has been embraced by many people enduring hardship. It is an inspirational closing poem to read aloud at the end of this eighth session. Think about your life and how you wish to live now as a result of cancer. Here is an excerpt from Markova's poem:

I will not die an unlived life.
I will not live in fear
of falling or catching fire.
I choose to inhabit my days,
to allow my living to open me,
to make me less afraid,
more accessible ...

... to live so that which came to me as seed
goes to the next as blossom
and that which came to me as blossom,
goes on as fruit.

Suggested Format for Session Eight

GUIDED VISUALIZATION: FROM DARKNESS INTO LIGHT

The meditation is followed by five minutes of writing that describes the journey through darkness. Invite the circle to read aloud without response.

EXERCISE 1: THE QUESTIONS IN YOUR MIND

Use the poem by Elena Georgiou, "Questions in the Mind of the Poet as She Washes the Floors." Read the poem once through as a group, with each person reading one of the poet's questions. Now read it a second time, with everyone underlining the question that most interests them. Write for twenty minutes, using the question they have underlined—or one they would like to ask themselves—as their prompt. Read aloud and respond.

SHORT BREAK *(ten minutes)*

EXERCISE 2: HOW I WANT TO BE REMEMBERED

Give a copy of Marilyn Nelson's poem "Cover Photograph" to each person. Begin by laying out a number of magazines with different women pictured on the covers. Ask the group to call out descriptive words or the accomplishments of the women that they associate with their photographs. Next read Nelson's poem aloud. You might read it aloud as a group, with each person taking a stanza. Ask each person to think about how she would like to be remembered. Write for twenty minutes, followed by reading and response.

CLOSING POEM: "I WILL NOT DIE AN UNLIVED LIFE"
BY DAWNA MARKOVA

*Read the poem aloud before forming the closing circle.
Ask each participant to offer one small thing that they wish to incorporate into their daily lives as a result of living with cancer.*

CHAPTER NINE

RECLAIMING ONE'S SELF

Eventually you learn to live with the fear, the discomfort, the disfiguration. You just do it.

— CANDICE, writing group member

Guided Visualization: Talking Back to Cancer

Sit comfortably in your seat, finding a position to help your body relax. Close your eyes or soft-focus on a spot in front of you. Let your breathing gradually become deeper and fuller. Remember, as you inhale and exhale, how you are filling your lungs and blood vessels with fresh energy to fuel your body and mind, and as you exhale, how the tensions and distractions that accompanied you here subside. Feel your body softening and settling and your thoughts becoming freer. Give into the gentle rhythm of your breathing, lulling you into quiet and calm. Notice how images begin to float behind your eyes one after the other. You begin to see that you have come to a place of safety, where you are becoming stronger, surer, and ready for a new life. As you look around, you can see images of your past, your journey through cancer into recovery and healing. As you explore this place, you become aware of something moving toward you in the distance—something you have known, and before now, feared. Look closely. It is the image of your cancer. Slowly now, move toward it, knowing you have the courage to confront it directly. If you feel your body tighten, take a moment and concentrate again on your breathing.

Remember that you are in a place of safety and support. Feel again the strength within you. Go toward the image of cancer. Imagine it taking on a personality or becoming a character. Look it squarely in the eyes. You have something you want to say to your cancer. Talk to it now. Tell it what you feel. Let it respond. Talk back to your cancer. Listen to the dialogue between you. Then, when you are ready, turn away and walk again to the center of that safe place, noticing, as you do, how you feel. Rest there a moment. Gradually, feel yourself becoming aware of the outer world, and when you are ready, open your eyes and write for five minutes. What did you have to say to your cancer?

A Transition Back to Normal Life

Cancer, you are malignant
unpredictably mean
But there is an army of us . . .
working night and day to block your way
and I believe some day
we'll prevail.

—NELI, writing group member

Cancer marks you in a particular way for the rest of your life. Yet you still have to go on living. In her book *The Breast Cancer Companion,* author Kathy LaTour discusses the process of becoming a cancer survivor. During the mid-eighties, a cancer survivorship movement began to emerge in the United States. Owing to advances in treatment and to early detections, people were surviving cancer in increasing numbers, asking questions, and becoming a visible community. What did it mean to be a cancer survivor? At a 1986 conference, Fitzhugh Mullan, a doctor and cancer survivor, described survival as beginning "when you are told you have cancer" and continuing for the rest of one's life. Laura's words echoed Dr. Mullan's. She said, "I will never move away from [cancer], even though I have an excellent prognosis. Cancer has, rather, moved me into a new phase of life."

You are now looking forward to your cancer treatments ending and to getting on with your life. However, the post-treatment period is also is a time of change and readjustment. Now the task is to assimilate the cancer experience into your life. It requires you to move beyond the anger, sorrow, and any lingering or unresolved issues. This readjustment doesn't happen overnight. For months, surgeries, treatments, and recovery have been uppermost in your mind, and as treatment comes to an end, you face whatever comes next. What was normal for you before cancer may not be normal for you now. In the months of change that accompany recovery, you must redefine what "normal" means. "Moving on is a challenge," Paula said. "Now what?"

After treatment, you might find that your expectations of yourself or of family and friends need readjusting. Both the disease and its treatment take their toll on you physically and emotionally. Your emotional recovery from cancer can take longer than your physical recovery. Everyone reacts differently; while fatigue or depression lingers for some, it doesn't for others. Regardless of the details of their experience, many women report that they need a few months to readjust and rethink what they want to accomplish in the next chapter of life.

After her treatment ended, Charlene slowly began to feel better, but "sometimes," she added, "it seemed impossibly slow." Nevertheless, as she came to terms with some of the inevitable physical changes after treatment, she said, "I feel more satisfied with my life. I look forward to gaining flexibility in dealing with my new circumstances."

The experience of cancer can also serve to strengthen your beliefs in your ability to cope. Margaret was emphatic about what she had learned from her illness: "It is imperative to reclaim your life and move on ... to utilize the coping skills, knowledge and personal growth ... and address the rest of your life with the same perseverance," she said.

Genel, who is an ICU nurse as well as a cancer survivor, wrote, "Often the best thing to do is to let go and just live. I have had to make some big decisions on my own and have gained confidence in my judgment." Judy agreed, saying, "I feel more in control of my life than I did before breast cancer."

Writing about Life, Not Just Cancer

There is little doubt that having cancer leaves an indelible imprint on your life, and yet, as you continue to write about your experience, your writing begins to shift. Cancer gradually becomes part of the fabric of your whole life. While it is always present, it gradually recedes from prominence in the writing that you do or that a writing group does together.

As the weeks progress and you begin to reclaim your life, memories and topics not related to cancer will begin to appear in your writing. If you are writing with a group, you'll hear voices grow stronger; tears will diminish, and laughter will be interwoven with shared memories. During this passage from pain into possibility and woundedness into healing, the joy of writing and telling your life stories becomes apparent. Your writing may shift from writing *for* your life to writing *about* your life, and that brings with it a special poignancy, joy, and vibrancy. Memories of first loves, first dates, first bicycles, parents, playmates, childhood homes, or children find their way onto paper. In a group, the bonds between the participants strengthen in the intimacy of shared stories.

In one of my earlier writing groups, Carol, diagnosed with metastatic breast cancer, wrote about her Illinois childhood and a memory of one steep hill she sledded down in the winter. When she returned to Illinois as an adult, however, she had discovered that the steep hill of her childhood memory barely had any incline! Everyone laughed as she read aloud and shared her surprise. "I love this group," she exclaimed. "We're not just writing about cancer; we're writing about life!"

Cancer *is* a significant chapter in our life stories, and, as Alice Hoffman has written, it informs those that follow. "I'll tell you the honest truth," said Tanya, a breast cancer survivor photographed for Art Myers's *Winged Victory.* "I would not undo this gift of perspective, even to have my breast back."

Sadly, cancer may be the final chapter of some members' lives. Nevertheless, as you heal emotionally, your desire to remember and write about your whole life increases. It is a way of saying, "This is my life. I have lived." Honoring your full life is deeply affirming and healing. "Having a life," Susan Sontag wrote, "is about tragedy and sorrow as much as it is about joy and contentment." Writing honors the full range of human experience as nothing else does.

EXERCISE 1: A SECOND CHANCE

Two years ago, Kathy Dunn, a colleague of mine from Amherst Writers & Artists, introduced an exercise using Rita Dove's inspirational poem "Dawn Revisited." Since then, I have incorporated it into every cancer writing group I have led. Dove's poem is a wonderful prompt for considering new possibilities. Here is an excerpt:

Imagine you wake up
with a second chance: The blue jay
hawks his pretty wares
and the oak still stands, spreading
glorious shade. If you don't look back,

the future never happens

If you are writing in a group, this will be a two-part exercise. Everyone should have a copy of the poem. Read the poem aloud to the group, then ask what they liked about the poem or what it suggests to them. Now read it a second time and have everyone underline the line they liked best. For the next portion of this exercise, you'll be re-creating Dove's poem.

Begin by having each person read aloud the line she has underlined. Encourage everyone to keep the rhythm and flow of the poem as you read. Does it still sound like poetry? Why? Invariably what takes shape is an interesting repetition of certain lines and fresh couplings of poetic lines, a piece of writing that is musical, joyous, and alive.

Now use the phrase you have underlined from Dove's poem as your writing prompt, and write for twenty minutes. This exercise has proven to be popular with every group I've led. It encourages everyone to look ahead, beyond their experience of cancer, but it also stimulates playfulness and fresh imagery in writing.

Pam chose the line "the whole sky is yours to write on" and wrote the following:

Cancer has claimed one year of my life, and in that year, I have moved from "victim" to "survivor." Like an invading army, it occupied me and dictated the terms of my existence. Now, having won the fight, I survey the battlefield that is my life and think about what I have left behind. . . .

The future is unclear, but I didn't know what the past would be either, when that was the future. And it turned out pretty good. Time to dust off the old dreams and invent some new.

When your life has been turned upside down, it's time to think inside out. If it's true that the whole sky is there to write on, there there's a lot yet to be said.

Helen used the metaphor of a bicycle race in looking toward her future:

"Pace yourself," I tell myself. "Remember what's ahead."
The hum of tires on pavement is pure music.
Today I am ready for the challenge.
Pedaling, pushing, wheels spinning ever faster.

The Healing Power of Humor

As he described in his memorable book *The Anatomy of an Illness,* Norman Cousins used laughter to deal with his own disease and pain. A sense of humor is also a crucial part of your ability to heal from cancer. Even though cancer is a painful and serious matter, humor provides relief from taking yourself so seriously. Not only does laughter have physical benefits, but sharing it helps you get outside yourself and to see the world a little differently; it lightens your spirit. You feel better. Laughter *is* good medicine.

Kathy LaTour, consulting senior editor for *CURE* magazine, turned her cancer experience into a one-woman comedy show. Her performance of *One Mutant Cell* has now been featured at a number of national conferences. Part journal excerpts written during her treatment and part commentary on some of her odd and humorous experiences after diagnosis, LaTour's rendition of her journey allows us to laugh with her *and* at our own experience.

Sharing laughter in the context of a writing group is an important aspect of the healing potential of writing together, and there are numerous ways to introduce writing about the more humorous aspects of everyone's lives into the sessions.

For example, when I introduced a simple prompt to write about a first—a first date, a first party dress, a first haircut—Varda, one of the writing group members, entertained everyone with a humorous account of a date with two brothers!

The Bernstein twins were an oddity of nature. Harold, the older brother by five minutes, was well over six feet tall and so thin he looked as though he'd been sliced in half lengthwise. Herbert, the younger twin ... bore a striking resemblance to Tweedle Dee.

Both brothers pursued me until I could not remember who was on the phone ... I was thirteen at the time; the twins were sixteen.

My mother despaired about my looks. "Nothing delicate about her. She's not graceful, and she's not clever," she confided to my aunt Bea, "but she's got great breasts."

"Those breasts will catch a man," she promised me as she pushed my unmanageable dark bangs out of my eyes ...

In the fall of my freshman year, both Bernsteins asked me to the homecoming dance. My mother was positively gleeful. But how could I choose between twin brothers—twins I could barely tolerate?

I eventually accepted both dates. ... I had a surprisingly enjoyable evening and found that a legend builds up around a girl with two corsages, two dates, and a great pair of breasts. And to my mother's delight, I was never without a date on weekends.

EXERCISE 2: WHAT WOMEN WANT

For this exercise, you will undoubtedly find your own favorite poem or prompt to inspire some spirited writing. There are many possibilities. One is Kim Addonizio's poem "What Do Women Want?" which describes the narrator's burning desire for a sexy red dress:

I want a red dress
I want it flimsy and cheap,
I want it too tight, I want to wear it
Until someone tears it off me

The narrator's lusty desire builds to a final line that will certainly produce a smile as you read:

and I'll wear it like bones, like skin,
it'll be the goddamned
dress they bury me in.

Read the poem aloud and underline or put an asterisk by the lines you like best, noticing the tone of the poem. Think about what you most enjoyed most in the poem, then write, asking yourself, "What do I really want? If I could have anything I wanted as a woman, what would it be?" Write for twenty minutes.

Marcia had already realized her desire for a red dress. In her poem she describes the dress she wore after her breast surgery, her Christmas party dress was:

Fire engine red
Maraschino cherry red
In-your-face-with-no-apology red . . .

Backless,
Allowing no bra to equalize my quite uneven breasts
But no matter.
I was alive,
and I danced.

An alternative to Addonizio's poem is "God Says Yes to Me" by Kaylin Haught. This poem is a humorous comment on the spirit of women, and a good reminder to let yourself be daring, to have fun, and to take risks. Here is an excerpt:

I asked God if it was okay to be melodramatic
And she said yes . . .

I asked her if I could wear nail polish
or not wear nail polish

and she said honey
she calls me that sometimes

she said you can do just exactly
what you want to . . .

what I'm telling you is
Yes Yes Yes

After you read the poem aloud, think about what you would give yourself permission to do or be if nothing stood in your way, then write for twenty minutes, keeping your pen moving rapidly across the paper.

You can also use some of the many different sets of women's card decks available commercially for this second exercise. Among those I have found most successful are the game cards from *Cowgirls Ride the Trail of Truth* (SideSaddle L.L.C. Cowgirls) and those from the deck *Celebrating Wild Women* (Conari Press). If you use cards like these, you can use Addonizio's or Haught's poems to set the stage, then draw one of the cards and use it as your writing prompt. Each of these resources invites you to be playful and feisty, the true goals of this exercise. The shared laughter in a writing group is certain to send everyone home with smiles on their faces.

A Closing Poem: The Cancer Patient Talks Back

In this ninth session, the resilience of the human spirit is apparent in the writers' ability to honor their whole life, to look to the future, and to laugh together, even in the face of cancer. As you end this session, read Molly Redmond's poem "The Cancer Patient Talks Back," published in *The Cancer Poetry Project*. Redmond's poem reflects the determination and resiliency that can now be heard in everyone's writing. She concludes by declaring:

But the only person I want to hear about
is your Grandma Ruth,
who was diagnosed at fifty
and died at ninety,
skydiving.

Otherwise,
hold your tongue.

Preparing for the Final Session

In the next chapter, I describe a closing ritual of sharing gratitude. In preparation for this ritual, give everyone a list of the group members' names and enough three-by-five cards for everyone in the group. Instruct the group to write short appreciative notes about each person's writing on the card and to sign their names. These gratitude cards will be collected at the beginning of the next meeting and distributed to the group at the closing of the final meeting.

Suggested Format for Session Nine

GUIDED VISUALIZATION: TALKING BACK TO CANCER

The meditation is followed by five minutes of writing.
Invite the circle to read aloud without response.

EXERCISE 1: A SECOND CHANCE
READ RITA DOVE'S "DAWN REVISITED"

aloud to the group. Read it a second time, instructing participants
to underline the line that they like best. Now read again, inviting
each person to read her favorite line aloud, as if you were doing a
group reading of a complete poem. Discuss the results with the group.
Finally, using their favorite line from Dove's poem, everyone writes
for twenty minutes. Read aloud and respond.

SHORT BREAK *(ten minutes)*

EXERCISE 2: WHAT WOMEN WANT

Using either Kim Addonizio's poem "What Do Women Want?"
or Kaylin Haught's "God Says Yes to Me," read the poem aloud,
asking for comments and reactions from the group. Ask the group
to write about what they really want or what they would like to give
themselves permission to do or be if they could. Write for twenty minutes,
followed by reading and response.

CLOSING POEM: "THE CANCER PATIENT TALKS BACK"
BY MOLLY REDMOND

Each person should have a copy of the poem. Read it aloud together,
with each person reading three lines. In your closing circle,
thank the group for their gifts of honesty, stories, poetry, and laughter.

CHAPTER TEN

THE LESSONS OF CANCER

Every day is a celebration of life.

—JANICE, writing group member

Guided Visualization: Who Am I Now?

Sit comfortably in your chair, and close your eyes or soft-focus on a spot on the floor. Let your body relax as you feel your spine firm against the chair back and your feet solidly on the floor, and rest your hands on your thighs, palms facing up and open. Begin by breathing deeply and slowly, in and out, in and out, establishing a gentle rhythm of inhales and exhales. As you breathe in, be aware of the flow of fresh oxygen that fuels your body and mind, and as you breathe out, release any remaining tensions or distractions. Focus inside, experiencing the peacefulness and quiet there. Know that you are safe among friends. Feel their warmth and acceptance. Now begin to float free, moving over the landscape of your life. Slowly, make your way back to that first day, that first time you heard the word cancer. *Remember the person you were then, on that day. Notice the sensations in your body, and then move forward, gradually retracing the memories and images from your journey through cancer ... the moments that were difficult; the moments when you felt loved and supported; the gradual changes in your body and spirit; the slow journey to recovery and healing, and now, the reemergence into a new life. See yourself now, someone who has lived through cancer, who may be living with cancer, who may now be cancer-free. Study this person. Feel admiration, gratitude, and love for her strength and her courage. Notice how she looks, how she feels, who she has become. Linger there with her for a few moments. . . . Then very slowly, make your way back into the outer world, this room, and this circle of friends, carrying the image of that person with you. When you are ready, open your eyes and, for the next five minutes, describe who you have become as a person who has experienced cancer.*

What Cancer Teaches Us

"Breast cancer, like any other illness, is one of life's teachers," Deb Haney said in her interview for Barbara Delinsky's book *Uplift.* "What do we take away from it? That depends on each of us. We can't change our situation, but we can make the most of it."

How can you make the most of your experience? What lessons or opportunities for learning has cancer provided? None of us would ever choose to be diagnosed with cancer; few would choose to undergo the discomfort and ordeal of treatment. And yet, cancer, like so many of the challenges life presents to us, can be a great teacher.

In her memorable poem "If I Had My Life to Live Over," Erma Bombeck, who died from breast cancer, wrote about what she had learned: "Mostly, given another shot at life, I would seize every minute . . . look at it and really see it . . . live it . . . and never give it back."

Author and journalist Stan Goldberg, reflecting on his bout with prostate cancer in an article for *USA Today,* wrote: "Cancer is painful, frightening, and tragically affects many. But it's also something else. It's a teacher. If we listen carefully, we can learn to live more fully and, ironically, to die better. I would have preferred a wise and compassionate uncle, but I didn't get one. Instead, I received lessons so simple and pure that they will continue to influence me throughout my life."

Time and again, people who have written with me during their illness say that their lives are permanently altered by the experience. Many discover the desire to redefine who they are and how they want to live. The changes may be small or great, but the lessons of cancer leave a lasting impression on a person's soul and spirit. "Breast cancer gave me a gift in exchange for the two precious breasts it took," Candice said. "I learned how to receive, and that's a lesson well learned and precious in its own right."

Liane sent an exuberant message to her email group at the end of her treatment, saying, "If you told me when I was first diagnosed that having breast cancer would be one of the best things that happened to me, I would have given you one of my 'evil' looks. . . . Now . . . I'm beginning to see the truth in that statement. . . . I can see that there are doors open to opportunities which are just waiting for me to embrace."

Susie, recently finished with her chemotherapy, said, "I now try to take each day at a time and not do a million things. I prioritize more. My first priority is to listen to my body."

Reflecting on the Experience of Cancer

As you near the end of this book and, perhaps, a writing group series, you have the chance to reflect on the experience of cancer. You've explored your cancer journey through writing for many weeks. In that time, evidence of your physical and emotional healing has become apparent, although group members may be at different stages of their recovery, depending on the nature and treatment of their cancers. Some may even be dealing with a recurrence, and yet, in the safety and support of a writing group, can express and share this setback in written words.

Jean, who died after a long struggle with colorectal cancer, wrote about what her writing group had given to her: "[It] helped me find my long hidden voice and . . . to sing again. Without [it] I would have buried my sorrow, my pain. . . . The warmth and kindness . . . brought me out of the darkness of a . . . terminal diagnosis."

At the final session of a writing series, it's important to articulate the movement from illness into healing, and from spiritual woundedness into wholeness. It is a chance to celebrate life. It is also a time to remember how far you have traveled in the many weeks of writing together. Honoring your journey and celebrating the return to a life fully lived is a vital ritual of healing.

If you are leading a writing group for people living with cancer, you'll quickly develop your own rituals for the final session of your series. In my own groups, our special activities have included sharing potluck suppers, incorporating visual art, such as handmade masks and book, into our writing, and, for anyone transitioning out of the writing group, holding a candle-lighting ceremony.

In my occasional collaboration with Heidi Darr-Hope, artist-in-residence at the South Carolina Cancer Center in Columbia, we have developed and co-led workshops that weave words together with images, combining writing with collage or with the creation of mandalas. Exploring the interplay between words images has been a powerful and moving experience both for the cancer patients and for us.

Showing Gratitude to Each Other

The final group session is also an opportunity to show your appreciation for one another. You have spent many weeks sharing heartache and joy, stories and poems, and have developed a strong bond of belonging and friendship. What can you do to show your gratitude? Here's one suggestion that comes from the Amherst Writers & Artists' method.

Remember what it felt like to get valentines from your classmates every February 14? How eagerly you waited to take your box of valentines home and read each one? Remember also how you chose each valentine carefully for its message, writing in your best penmanship "To Annie," "To Billy," and carefully signing your name?

This closing ritual of gratitude has its roots in that early valentine ritual and is a way to express the gratitude you feel for other retreats and workshops, such as leadership training, creativity, or writing. When you use it as a closing activity in a cancer writing group, you can affirm the beauty of and your gratitude for each person's writing and contribution to the group.

You will have given everyone the necessary materials at the close of your ninth meeting: a list of the participants' names and enough colored three-by-five cards for each person in the group, with the instructions that "valentines" will be shared at the final session. Everyone writes a note of appreciation or remembrance of their colleagues' writing on the cards, signing their name at the bottom. I always like to remind my groups to complete their valentines a few days before our final meeting.

Before group members arrive, place paper lunch bags or large envelopes, labeled with each person's name, on a table. As people arrive, they will place their valentines in the bags before you begin the first exercise. At the close of the meeting, each person will have her own envelope of valentines to take home and read, with the joy of being and writing together wonderfully affirmed.

EXERCISE 1: THE LESSONS OF CANCER

What lessons has cancer offered to you at this point in your journey? Begin this exercise by first reading Judy Rohm's poem "A Lesson," one of the many cancer poems in the award-winning *The Cancer Poetry Project.* Here is an excerpt:

because cancer teaches that snorkeling
coral reefs pays greater dividends than a savings account
and mowing summer grass can be postponed
for bike rides past wild flowers and country streams ...
Cancer is not a gift but a lesson
full of seeing now and loving presently.

Take a few moments to respond to any part of the poem that particularly appeals to you. Take some time to reflect on the lessons that you have learned from the cancer experience, and for twenty minutes, begin writing. You might want to start with the line "Cancer is not a gift, but a lesson" and write from there.

Shortly after Sally was diagnosed with breast cancer, her husband discovered he had prostate cancer. The experiences they shared brought them closer together. In a short piece she titled "Lessons Learned," she wrote: "I learned that what I had, breast cancer, and what he had, prostate cancer, could be conquered. And that together, we could help each other overcome this nasty impediment lurking in the corner of our lives, waiting to take us from the golden sunset years ahead of us. . . . I have learned that we can count on the vows we took years ago that bind us through sickness and health."

Kristen, who was still reeling from the discovery of another tumor in her breast, questioned what she had learned:

I thought cancer had taught me to
Be strong, to endure, to persevere. But
That wasn't enough ...

I thought I had learned patience
One day at a time, slow and steady ...
But that wasn't enough ...

As she continued to write, she gradually moved toward resolution:

Maybe then, the lesson is freedom.
Freedom of mind and of heart.
Freedom to just live
inside out
with open soul
unburdened
unhampered
today, tomorrow.
I will, I do, I did.

Pam wrote about what she had learned, remembering an issue of a magazine she'd read one October, Breast Cancer Awareness Month. It featured several courageous cancer survivors, including someone who had climbed a mountain in the midst of chemotherapy. Pam expressed a pang of guilt as she read of their achievements and asked, "What I am doing with my life?" She wrote honestly about the lessons she had learned from her cancer: "I've learned I can't do everything. I have limits ... I've learned that energy is a precious commodity, not to be squandered on things that don't matter.... I've learned that I'm not the only person I can count on.... I've learned that I don't want to turn my back on my old life.... Is that wrong?"

Nancy, a single mother of seven-year-old triplets, reflected on her experience in a short poem entitled "Cancer's Lessons":

At the Relay for Life I
finally
feel like a survivor.
I cry to see all the other
survivors
and their friends.
Is the lesson about
patience and joy, God?
Please let me learn it right
now.

Cancer teaches us many things: to take care of our health, to pay attention to the small gifts of each day, to be open to receiving as well as to giving. It also teaches us humility. Peggy wrote about her realization of others' pain and struggles as she finally walked across the Golden Gate Bridge just six weeks after her surgery: "And now I know, after traveling my journey and opening my ears and heart to the stories of those who will tell them, that most people on the bridge carried their own private burdens and sadness. I just didn't know it at the time."

Ann, also recovering from breast cancer, wrote a moving essay she titled "Lessons Learned." Here is an excerpt:

I have learned to treat each day as if it were the last, as each moment is precious.... I learned that there are no books on how to live; it's up to each of us to write our own.... I learned that the act of forgiving begins in ourselves. I learned that the sound of the wind and the lap of the waves are beautiful music.... I learned to slow down and enjoy the solitude of being myself.... I learned that the wound can be felt, but it can also be healed.... I learned to love my body even though it has cancer.... I have learned about truth, love, and friendship. Here, now.

EXERCISE 2: THE JOURNEY INTO HEALING

Several years ago, as I was training to be a bereavement counselor, the group leader passed around a large, sharp-edged stone, saying that our grief, when we first lose someone, is much like the stone: heavy, because our pain is raw and so sharply felt. Then he gave us a smaller, smoother stone, telling us that as we begin to heal from the loss of a loved one, we still carry the memory within us, but the grief is less burdensome, and the raw edges of sorrow have smoothed. Those stones, the weight and the feel of them in my hands, have stayed with me, providing the inspiration for a writing exercise I now use routinely in every final session of my writing groups.

In "Bridges," her final poem in a collection of cancer poetry *Reading the Body*, Caryn Mirriam-Goldberg writes:

I do not have words big enough for how far I traveled.
I do not have language intimate enough
for how I arrived here, to the world more itself
than it ever was before

Though it may be difficult to find the words to describe your journey through cancer, trying to express it fully often produces writing that glistens with beauty and power. Using a stone—forged from fiery and turbulent beginnings and becoming an object of smooth beauty and symmetry—as a metaphor is an exercise that can inspire you to describe just how far you have traveled.

For this final exercise, you'll need one large stone, the size of a small orange, rough and sharp to the touch. You'll also need an assortment of small river stones or smooth pebbles from the beach. If you lack a beach or a riverfront, most garden shops offer bags of small stones for flower arranging, and those will work nicely.

Pass the rough, heavy stone to each participant, describing how, in moments of loss or hardship, emotions are raw, often piercing and sharply felt. After each person has held and felt the larger stone, pass around a basket of the smaller, smooth stones. Invite each person to take one. These stones can be symbolic of the journey of life, and the journey of cancer: how our lives are marked by times of struggle, pain, or loss as well joy. The small stones have been worn down, tossed and turned by oceans and rivers over time, transformed from jagged pieces of rock to something smooth and soothing to the touch. Yet at their core, they retain the soul of who they have always been.

Examine the small stone you have chosen for yourself. As you hold it, notice all the detail in it, imagining its journey out of those ancient, volatile beginnings and into the smooth, round stone it has become. Using the stone as your metaphor, write about your journey through cancer. Allow twenty-five minutes. If you are writing with others, you may read aloud, but do so without response, simply holding each person's words in quiet appreciation. At the end of this exercise I like to offer the stones to each person to take home as a sort of talisman and a reminder of their journey and transformation.

The writing produced by this exercise is always touching and powerful. You may be starting to experience resolution, or you might feel that you have only just begun to discover the meaning of your cancer experience and its place in your life.

In a piece she called "Journey into a Dark Place," Carolyn wrote about the first moment she was diagnosed, just before September 11, 2001, and her subsequent journey into recovery, as she sought to make sense of her struggle:

At this point in the heroic story, the formula requires that I tell you how my life has been transformed by cancer; how I have become a better person with reordered priorities, that I now take time to smell the flowers, that my experience of life-threatening disease has changed me into a better human being. And I have to confess that at first I believed this and looked for a brave new life to reveal itself to me. . . . Like all those waiting to hear the good news after September 11, I, too, still wait.

Ceci used her stone to inspire a short piece that she titled "The Cycle of Life," which signaled her acceptance of her experience and the strength of her faith.

We travel a full circle in our life's journey here on earth. We start out helpless, needy, and dependent on others. And if we're fortunate to mature to full cycle, we once again become helpless, needy, and dependent. Those of us who have shortened life spans will reach this stage sooner than others. I guess this is just nature's way of recycling—we start off crying as we emerge from our mother's womb, and later, we return peacefully once again into the womb of God.

Laura described herself as having "crossed the boundary line of the risky circle of cancer":

As I cross into this new country,
I meet fellow countrywomen who also didn't choose
to come to this place.
We wave to one another across roads and fields
as we go along our own way,
still living our lives, but in this strange new land.

Carol, who looked back across the landscape of her own journey, acknowledged her healing:

My heart is gently opening.
I let in the joy.
I let in the pain.
I let in LIFE.

A Closing Poem: Song

There are so many poems to choose from for your reading at this final session; "Song," written by Kevin Smith, and published in *The Cancer Poetry Project,* is one of my favorites. Smith is a psychologist who watched his mother deal with breast cancer and a mastectomy. She ultimately became cancer-free, and his poem ends on a note of hope and celebration. After describing a woman entering the hospital intact but emerging with only one breast after surgery, he asks:

Then when she caresses
Her naked body
Will she hear all or half
The sparrow's sad song?

No
She will open
her mouth and
Sing a song
Of life.

Give everyone a copy of the poem so they may follow along. Read it aloud to the group, repeating the last stanza once before moving into your closing circle.

The Closing Circle: A Celebration of Women

As you end this final session, you may wish to introduce another Native American chant that involves everyone's participation. "The Osage Woman's Initiation Song," from *Women in Search of the Sacred*, was once sung at the end of Osage women's initiation rites. In their culture, the women were responsible for planting, cultivating, and harvesting corn. The ritual of planting and cultivating was at the center of life. This song honors the life-giving role of women and its sacredness in the world. As in the traditional Navajo prayer introduced earlier in this book, chanting and repetition are used to call forth order in the world. Here is an excerpt from the original poem, translated by Francis La Flesche:

I have made a footprint, a sacred one.
I have made a footprint; through it the blades push upward.
I have made a footprint, through it the blades radiate.
... I have made a footprint; I live in the light of day.

Read the poem aloud together, with each person reciting one line. As leader, read the entire poem a second time. Now, as you stand in the circle, each person will say one sentence of her own, beginning with "I have made a footprint ..." then adding a statement of identity, such as, "I have made a footprint, my children live in love," or "I have made a footprint, my stories are legacies of my life."

Whatever each person feels moved to say defines this act of collaborative poem making. When everyone has spoken, add your closing statement, for example, "We have made our footprints; we live in the light of day." Adjourn, thanking everyone for the gifts of all the weeks of shared stories and poems, and then extinguish the candle flame.

It is at the final session of a writing series that you will be most aware of the healing power of writing. Whenever I look around the circle of writers at a final meeting, I see evidence of healing in each person's smiling face. I remember how each one came to the first session, wounded and in distress about her diagnosis, weakened and dispirited from the ordeal of treatment. As the weeks go by, the shared stories and poems reveal how each person's voice grows in strength, depth, and beauty. The bonds of community and friendship are unmistakable. I feel honored to witness and share in their journeys, their hardships and joys. As I look at the women's faces around the closing circle, my heart is full. This is the power of our words to heal. This is the joyous work of leading a writing group for people who live with cancer. This is the experience of writing together through cancer, which I offer to you here.

Suggested Format for Session Ten

Distributing Group "Valentines"

Place lunch bags or envelopes labeled with each person's name on a table.
As the participants arrive, they should place their "valentines" for each group
member in the appropriate bag. These will be passed out at the end of the session.

Guided Visualization: Who Am I Now?

The meditation is followed by five minutes of writing. Invite the circle
to read aloud without response.

EXERCISE 1: THE LESSONS OF CANCER

Use the poem "A Lesson" by Judy Rohm as the prompt for the exercise, giving everyone a copy so that they can follow along as you read it aloud to the group. Encourage responses to the lines or images in the poem. Ask the group to reflect on the lessons of their own cancer experience and to write for twenty minutes. You can suggest that they use the line "Cancer is not a gift but a lesson" from Rohm's poem as a starting point. Invite reading aloud and group response.

SHORT BREAK *(ten minutes)*

EXERCISE 2: THE JOURNEY INTO HEALING

You'll need an apple-sized rough stone and a basket of small, smooth stones. Pass the rough stone around the circle, commenting on how emotions are raw and ragged when we are first diagnosed. Pass around the smoother stone, observing that gradually our emotions smooth out and become more manageable, even though the experience of cancer is always with us. Now pass around the river stones, inviting each person to choose one and to use it as the metaphor for their own journey of healing. Write for twenty-five minutes, followed by reading and response. Members can take the stones home as a reminder of their journey.

CLOSING POEM: "SONG" BY KEVIN SMITH

Give everyone a copy of the poem. Read it aloud once, and then repeat the last stanza. Allow a few moments of silence, and then move into your closing circle.

CLOSING CIRCLE: THE OSAGE WOMAN'S INITIATION SONG

Read the poem aloud together, with each person reciting one line and with you, as leader, ending with "I have made a footprint; I walk in the light of day." Now create a new song as a group, with each person repeating the line "I have made a footprint" and then adding her own words, and move once more around the circle. When it's your turn, end the chant with the beginning line, "We have made our footprints . . ." and add your own words. Adjourn. The group members can take their bags of "valentines" as they leave.

POETRY RESOURCES
for Writing Exercises

CHAPTER 1. WRITING TOGETHER FOR THE FIRST TIME

Hikmet, Nazim. "This Journey." In *Poems of Nazim Hikmet*. Translated by Randy Blasing and Mutlu Konuk. New York: Persea Books, 1994.

Oliver, Mary. "The Journey." In *Dreamwork: New and Selected Poems*. Boston: Beacon Press, 1992.

Rotella, Alexis. "Purple." In *Step Lightly: Poems for the Journey*, ed. Nancy Willard. San Diego: Harcourt Brace, 1998.

Walcott, Derek. "Love after Love." In *Collected Poems 1948–1984*. New York: Farrar, Straus & Giroux, 1986.

CHAPTER 2. WHEN THE DOCTOR SAYS, "CANCER"

Carver, Raymond. "Fear." In *All of Us*. New York: Knopf, 1996.

Clifton, Lucille. "1994." In *The Terrible Stories*. Rochester, NY: BOA Editions, 1996.

Halperin, Joan. "Diagnosis." In *Her Soul Beneath the Bone: Women's Poetry on Breast Cancer*, ed. Leatrice H. Lifshitz. Urbana: University of Illinois Press, 1998.

Ryan, Kay. "Survival Skills." In *Say Uncle*. New York: Grove Press, 2000.

CHAPTER 3. TELLING FAMILY AND FRIENDS

Halperin, Joan. "Injunction." In *Her Soul Beneath the Bone: Women's Poetry on Breast Cancer*, ed. Leatrice H. Lifshitz. Urbana: University of Illinois Press, 1998.

Milosch, Joe. Untitled poem. In *Poetic Medicine: The Healing Art of Poem-Making*, ed. John Fox. New York: Tarcher/Putnam, 1997.

CHAPTER 4. UNDERGOING TREATMENTS

Alexanderson, Lauren. "When I Inherit the Star." In *The Cancer Poetry Project: Poems by Cancer Patients and Those Who Love Them*, ed. Karin B. Miller. Minneapolis: Fairview Press, 2001.

Kenyon, Jane. "Credo," from "Having It Out with Melancholy." In *Otherwise: New and Selected Poems*. St. Paul: Graywolf Press, 1996.

Metzger, Deena. "Healing." In *Her Soul Beneath the Bone: Women's Poetry on Breast Cancer,* ed. Leatrice H. Lifshitz. Urbana: University of Illinois Press, 1998.

CHAPTER 5. WRITING THE BODY

Clifton, Lucille. "Homage to my Hips." In *Good Woman: Poems and a Memoir.* Rochester, NY: BOA Editions, 1987.

_____. "Scar." In *The Terrible Stories.* Rochester, NY: BOA Editions, 1996.

Mirriam-Goldberg, Caryn, "Reading the Body." In *Reading the Body.* Lawrence, KS: Mammoth Press, 2004.

_____. "I Want to Tell You How Beautiful You Are." In *Reading the Body.* Lawrence, KS: Mammoth Press, 2004.

Nelson, Marilyn. "Cover Photograph." In *The Fields of Praise: New and Selected Poems.* Baton Rouge: Louisiana State University Press, 1994.

Ondaatje, Michael. "The Time Around Scars." In *The Cinnamon Peeler.* New York: Vintage Books: 1991.

CHAPTER 6. FINDING SUPPORT

Jane Kenyon. "Let Evening Come." In *Otherwise: New and Selected Poems.* St. Paul: Graywolf Press, 1996.

CHAPTER 7. FAITH AND SPIRITUALITY

Marshock, Patti. "Gifts." In *The Cancer Poetry Project: Poems by Cancer Patients and Those Who Love Them,* ed. Karin B. Miller. Minneapolis: Fairview Press, 2001.

Robison, Margaret. "What Matters, Then?" In *Red Creek, a Requiem.* Amherst, MA: Amherst Writers & Artists Press, 1992.

"Traditional Navajo Prayer." In *Women in Praise of the Sacred: 43 Centuries of Spiritual Poetry by Women,* ed. Jane Hirshfield. New York: HarperCollins, 1994.

CHAPTER 8. RECURRENCE AND DEATH

Georgiou, Elena. "Questions in the Mind of the Poet as She Washes the Floors." In *Mercy, Mercy Me*. Madison: University of Wisconsin Press, 2000.

Nelson, Marilyn. "Cover Photograph." In *The Fields of Praise: New and Selected Poems*. Baton Rouge: Louisiana State University Press, 1994.

Markova, Dawna. "I Will Not Die an Unlived Life." In *I Will Not Die An Unlived Life: Reclaiming Purpose and Passion*. Boston: Conari Press, 2000.

CHAPTER 9. RECLAIMING ONE'S SELF

Dove, Rita. "Dawn Revisited." In *Callaloo* 2, no. 1 (1999): 24.

Addonizio, Kim. "What Do Women Want?" In *Tell Me*. Rochester, NY: BOA Editions, 2000.

Haught, Kaylin. "God Says Yes to Me." In *In The Palm of Your Hand: The Poet's Portable Workshop,* ed. Steve Kowit. Gardiner, ME: Tilbury House, 1995

Redmond, Molly. "The Cancer Patient Talks Back." In *The Cancer Poetry Project: Poems by Cancer Patients and Those Who Love Them*, ed. Karin B. Miller. Minneapolis: Fairview Press, 2001.

CHAPTER 10. THE LESSONS OF CANCER

Rohm, Judy. "A Lesson." In *The Cancer Poetry Project: Poems by Cancer Patients and Those Who Love Them*, ed. Karin B. Miller. Minneapolis: Fairview Press, 2001.

Smith, Kevin. "Song." In *The Cancer Poetry Project: Poems by Cancer Patients and Those Who Love Them*, ed. Karin B. Miller. Minneapolis: Fairview Press, 2001.

"Osage Woman's Initiation Song." In *Women in Praise of the Sacred: 43 Centuries of Spiritual Poetry by Women*, ed. Jane Hirshfield. New York: HarperCollins, 1994.

BIBLIOGRAPHY

Achtenberg, Jeanne, Barbara Dossey, and Leslie Kolkmeier. *Rituals of Healing: Using Imagery for Health and Wellness.* New York: Bantam, 1994.

Adams, Kathleen. *Journal to the Self.* New York: Warner Books, 1990.

Addonizio, Kim. *Tell Me.* Rochester, NY: BOA Editions, 2000.

Albert, Susan W. *Writing from Life: A Guide to Telling the Soul's Story for Women on an Inward Way.* New York: Tarcher/Putnam, 1997.

Anderson, Charles M., and Marion M., MacCurdy, eds. *Writing and Healing: Toward an Informed Practice.* Urbana, IL: National Council of Teachers of English, 2000.

Baldwin, Christina. *Life's Companion: Journal Writing as a Spiritual Quest.* New York: Bantam Books, 1991.

Barasch, Marc Ian. *The Healing Path: A Soul Approach to Illness.* New York: Penguin Books, 1993.

Bernard, Jamie. *Breast Cancer There and Back: A Woman-to-Woman Guide.* New York: Warner Books, 2001.

Bolen, Jean Shinoda, MD. *Close to the Bone: Life Threatening Illness and the Search for Meaning.* New York: Scribner, 1996.

Bolton, Gillie. *The Therapeutic Potential of Creative Writing: Writing Myself.* London: Jessica Kingsley Publishers, 1999.

Braude, Ted. "The Reach of the Mind: An Interview with Larry Dossey." *The Sun* 228 (December 1994): 3–9.

Bray, Sharon. *A Healing Journey: Writing Together Through Breast Cancer.* Amherst, MA: Amherst Writers & Artists Press, 2004.

Brennan, Murray F. "Dealing with the Fear of Recurrence." Available at www.psychooncology.net/dealing_with_the_fear_of_recurrence_body.html.

Broyard, Anatole. *Intoxicated by My Illness: And Other Writings on Life and Death.* New York: Ballantine, 1992.

Cameron, Julia. *The Artist's Way: A Spiritual Path to Higher Creativity.* New York: Tarcher/Putnam, 1992.

Campo, Rafael. *The Healing Art: A Doctor's Black Bag of Poetry.* New York: Norton, 2003.

Cancer as a Turning Point: From Surviving to Thriving (audiotapes). Boulder, CO: Sounds True Publishers, 2000.

Carver, Raymond. *All of Us.* New York: Vintage Books, 2000.

Clifton, Lucille. *Good Woman: Poems and a Memoir.* Rochester, NY: BOA Editions, 1987.

_____. *The Terrible Stories.* Rochester, NY: BOA Editions, 1996.

Cousins, Norman. *Anatomy of an Illness as Perceived by the Patient: Reflections on Healing and Regeneration.* New York: Bantam, 1979.

Delinsky, Barbara. *Uplift: Secrets from the Sisterhood of Breast Cancer Survivors.* New York: Pocket Books, 2001.

DeSalvo, Louise. *Writing as a Way of Healing: How Telling Our Stories Transforms Our Lives.* Boston: Beacon Press. 1999.

Dossey, Larry. *Healing Words: The Power of Prayer and the Practice of Medicine.* San Francisco: HarperSanFrancisco, 1993.

Dove, Rita, "Dawn Revisited." *Callaloo* 2, no. 1 (1999): 24

Driskill, Joseph. *Protestant Spiritual Exercises: Theology, History and Practice.* Harrisburg, PA: Morehouse Publishing, 1999.

Earle, Ralph. "At the Heart of Healing: An Interview with Stephen Levine." *The Sun* 167 (October 1989): 2–10.

Fox, John, ed. *Poetic Medicine: The Healing Art of Poem-Making.* New York: Tarcher/Putnam, 1997.

Foster, Patricia, and Mary Swander, eds. *The Healing Circle: Authors Writing of Recovery.* New York: Plume Books, 1998.

Frankl, Viktor. *Man's Search for Meaning.* Boston: Beacon Press, 2000.

Giorgiou, Elena. *Mercy, Mercy Me.* Madison: University of Wisconsin Press, 2000.

Goldberg, Natalie. *Wild Mind: Living the Writer's Life.* New York: Bantam, 1990.

Goldberg, Stan. "Cancer's Life Lessons." *USA Today,* April 12, 2005.

Hacker, Marilyn. *Winter Numbers: Poems.* New York: Norton, 1994.

Hampl, Patricia. *I Could Tell You Stories: Sojourns in the Land of Memory.* New York: Norton, 2000.

Hikmet, Nazim. *Poems of Nazim Hikmet.* Translated by Randy Blasing and Mutlu Konuk. New York: Persea Books, 1994.

Hirshfield, Jane, ed. *Women in Praise of the Sacred: 43 Centuries of Spiritual Poetry by Women.* New York: HarperCollins, 1994.

Hoffman, Alice. "Sustained by Fiction While Facing Life's Facts." *New York Times,* August 14, 2000.

Hoffman, Barbara. *A Cancer Survivor's Almanac: Charting Your Journey.* Hoboken, NJ: Wiley, 1996.

Jensen, Derrick. "Body Language: A Conversation with Marc Ian Barasch on Illness and Healing." *The Sun* 289 (January 2000): 4–13.

Kenyon, Jane. *Otherwise: New and Selected Poems, 1996.* St. Paul: Graywolf Press, 1996.

Kowit, Steve. *In The Palm of Your Hand: The Poet's Portable Workshop.* Gardiner, ME: Tilbury House Publishers, 1995.

LaTour, Kathy. *The Breast Cancer Companion.* New York: Avon Books, 1993.

Lepore, Stephen J., and Joshua M., Smyth, eds. *The Writing Cure: How Expressive Writing Promotes Health and Well-Being.* Washington DC: American Psychological Association, 2002.

LeShan, Lawrence. *Cancer as a Turning Point: A Handbook for People with Cancer, Their Families, and Health Professionals.* New York: Plume, 1994.

Levine, Stephen. *Guided Meditations, Explorations and Healings.* New York: Doubleday, 1991.

Lifshitz, Leatrice H., ed. *Her Soul Beneath the Bone: Women's Poetry on Breast Cancer.* Urbana: University of Illinois Press, 1998.

Lorde, Audrey. *The Cancer Journals.* New York: Spinsters Ink, 1980.

Markova, Dawna. *I Will Not Die an Unlived Life: Reclaiming Purpose and Passion.* Boston: Conari Press, 2000.

Martin, Chia. *Writing Your Way Through Cancer.* Prescott, AZ: Hohm Press, 2000.

Matuschka, "Why I Did It." *Glamour Magazine* (November 1993): 162.

Mayer, Musa. "Scribbling My Way to Spiritual Well-Being." *MAMM Magazine* (April, 2000): 26–29.

Metzger, Deena. *Writing for Your Life: Discovering the Story of Your Life's Journey.* San Francisco: HarperSanFrancisco, 1992.

Miller, Karin B., ed. *The Cancer Poetry Project: Poems by Cancer Patients and Those Who Love Them.* Minneapolis: Fairview Press, 2001.

Mirriam-Goldberg, Caryn. *Reading the Body.* Lawrence, KS: Mammoth Press, 2004.

Myers, Linda Joy. *Becoming Whole: Writing Your Healing Story.* San Diego: Silver Threads, 2003.

Myers, Art, and Maria Marrocchino. *Winged Victory: Altered Images: Transcending Breast Cancer.* San Diego: Photographic Gallery of Fine Art, 1996.

National Cancer Institute. "Spirituality in Cancer Care." Available at www.nci.nih.gov/cancertopics/pdq/supportivecare/spirituality/patient.

National Cancer Institute. "Loss, Grief and Bereavement." Available at www.cancer.gov/cancertopics/pdq/supportivecare/bereavement/healthprofessional

Nelson, Marilyn. *The Fields of Praise: New and Selected Poems.* Baton Rouge: Louisiana State University Press, 1994.

O'Connell, Nicholas. *At the Field's End: Interviews with 22 Pacific Northwest Writers.* Seattle: University of Washington Press, 1998.

Oliver, Mary. *New and Selected Poems.* Boston: Beacon Press, 1992.

Ondaatje, Michael. *The Cinnamon Peeler.* New York: Vintage Books, 1991.

Pennebaker, James W. *Opening Up: The Healing Power of Expressing Emotions.* New York: Guilford Press, 1997.

_____. "Writing About Emotional Experience as a Therapeutic Process." *Psychological Science* 8, no. 3 (1997): 162–66.

Pennebaker, James W., and Jane D. Segal. "Forming a Story: The Health Benefits of Narrative." *Journal of Clinical Psychology* 55, no. 10 (1999): 1243–54.

Pope, Robert. *Illness and Healing: Images of Cancer.* Hartsport, Nova Scotia: Lancelot Press, 1996.

Reider, Connie Zucker. *In Shadow and Light: Looking for the Gifts of Cancer.* Servana Park, MD: Bay Media. 2003.

Rico, Gabrielle. *Pain and Possibility: Writing Your Way Through Personal Crisis.* New York: Tarcher/Putnam, 1991.

Roberts, Larenda. "Writing for Their Lives." *Palo Alto Weekly,* November 14, 2001.

Robison, Margaret. *Red Creek, a Requiem.* Amherst MA: Amherst Writers & Artists Press, 1992.

Rossman, Martin L. *Fighting Cancer from Within: How to Use the Power of Your Mind For Healing.* New York: Henry Holt, 2003.

Ryan, Kay. *Say Uncle.* New York: Grove Press, 2000.

Schneider, Myra. *Writing My Way Through Cancer.* London: Jessica Kingsley Publishers, 2003.

Schneider, Pat. *Writing Alone and with Others.* New York: Oxford University Press, 2003.

_____. *Writing Alone and with Others: A Companion Piece to the Book* (DVD). Produced by Diane Garey and Larry Hott. Florentine Films, 2003.

Smolan, Rick, and Elliott, David. *A Day in the Life of America.* New York: HarperCollins, 1986.

Sontag, Susan. *Illness as Metaphor.* New York: Farrar, Straus and Giroux, 1978.

_____."The Risk Taker," an interview with Gary Younge, *The Guardian,* January 19, 2002.

Spann, Chip, ed. *Poet Healer: Contemporary Poems for Health and Healing.* Sacramento: Sutter's LAMP, 2004

Spiegel, David. *Living Beyond Limits.* New York: Ballantine, 1993.

_____. "Therapeutic Support Groups." In *Healing and the Mind,* ed. Bill Moyers, Sue Flowers, and David Grubin. New York: Doubleday, 1993.

Spiegel, David, and Catherine Classen. *Group Therapy for Cancer Patients: A Research-based Handbook of Psychosocial Care.* New York: Basic Books, 2000.

Stanton, Annette L. et al. "Randomized, Controlled Trial of Written Emotional Expression and Benefit Finding in Breast Cancer Patients." *Journal of Clinical Oncology* 20, no. 20 (2002): 4160–68.

Taylor, Daniel. *The Healing Power of Stories: Creating Yourself From the Stories of Your Life.* New York: Bantam Books, 1996.

Vecchione, Patrice. *Writing and the Spiritual Life: Finding Your Voice by Looking Within.* New York: McGraw Hill/Contemporary Books, 2001.

Walcott, Derek. *Collected Poems 1948–1984.* New York: Farrar, Strauss & Giroux, 1986.

Weiss, Marisa, MD, and Ellen Weiss. *Living Beyond Breast Cancer: A Survivor's Guide for When Treatment Ends and the Rest of Your Life Begins.* New York: Times Books, 1997.

Willard, Nancy, ed. *Step Lightly: Poems for the Journey.* San Diego: Harcourt Brace, 1998.

Zimmerman, Susan. *Writing to Heal the Soul: Transforming Grief and Loss Through Writing.* New York: Three Rivers Press, 2001.

SELECTED ORGANIZATIONS

American Cancer Society
Atlanta, GA 30329
800-228-4327
www.cancer.org

Amherst Writers & Artists
190 University Drive
Amherst, MA 01002
413-253-3307
www.amherstwriters.com

Arts and Healing Network
P.O. Box 276
Stinson Beach, CA 94970
www.artheals.org

**Center for
Autobiographic Studies**
P.O. Box 233
Sunland, CA 91041-0233
www.storyhelp.com

Center for Journal Therapy
1115 Grant Street, No. 207
Denver, CO 80203
888-421-2298
www.journaltherapy.com

**Goddard College, Transformative
Language Arts Program**
123 Pitkin Road
Plainfield, VT 05667
800-906-8312
www.goddard.edu/academic/TLAhtml

**National Association
for Poetry Therapy**
525 S.W. Fifth Street
Des Moines, IO 50309-4501
www.poetrytherapy.org

**National Cancer Institute
(National Institutes of Health)**
P.O. Box 24128
Baltimore, MD 21227
800-422-6237
www.cancer.gov

**New York University
Medical Humanities**
Literature, Arts & Medicine Database
http://endeavor.med.nyu.edu/lit-
med/medhum.html

The Society for Arts in Healthcare
2437 Fifteenth Street, N.W.
Washington, D.C. 20009
202-299-9887
www.thesah.org

ABOUT THE AUTHOR

Writer and teacher Sharon Bray holds a doctorate in Applied Psychology from the University of Toronto, completed the Writers' Program in Literary Fiction from the University of Washington, and studied Transformative Language Arts at Goddard College in Vermont and creative writing at the Humber School for Writers in Toronto, Canada. Her first book—a children's book—was published when she was a young mother living in Nova Scotia. She is also the author of *A Healing Journey: Writing Together Through Breast Cancer* (Amherst Writers & Artists Press, 2004), which chronicles her own experience with breast cancer and with leading writing groups for cancer survivors. Bray has written and published poetry, memoir, and a number of professional articles, and is featured on the DVD *Writing Alone & With Others* (Florentine Films) discussing her work with cancer survivors. She is a member of the Society for Arts in Healthcare, the American Psychological Association, Amherst Writers & Artists, National Association of Poetry Therapy, and is a Senior Fellow of the American Leadership Forum, Silicon Valley. Bray divides her time between the San Francisco Bay Area and San Diego, California.